The World's **First**
QUIP THESAURUS

with literally
Billions of Quips

and a Convenient RESOURCE FOR WRITERS when "Good Enough" Isn't

Caleb Spalding Atwood

authorHOUSE®

AuthorHouse™ LLC
1663 Liberty Drive
Bloomington, IN 47403
www.authorhouse.com
Phone: 1-800-839-8640

Published by AuthorHouse   10/10/2013

ISBN: 978-1-4918-1742-1 (sc)
ISBN: 978-1-4918-1741-4 (e)

Library of Congress Control Number: 2013917016

Table of Contents

INTRODUCTION

Have you ever heard a really clever quip, but quickly lost track of it? If so, I hate to break this to you, but you're normal. Odds are you've lost track of quips hundreds of times if you're young and thousands if you are "experienced" (i.e. old). I have and that led to writing down quips so clever, fascinating or bizarre I wished I had thought of them. My goal originally was to collect 1,000 and make them available for others who write, teach, train or speak publicly. According to Andy Hunt, author of *The Pragmatic Programmer*, the technical name for my effort should have been "R & D" (Rip off and Duplicate) although I did cite sources when traceable or recallable. Often, however, they were not so those who actually created them, or preceded me in "R & D" – must remain blameless.

In the process of collecting quips, I learned a great deal about how to create them. In 2010 this led the *Quip Factory, Millions of Quips, Rips, Dingers, Zingers and barbs – and how you can create thousands more*. The *Factory* was well regarded by many, including ForeWord Clarion Reviews, a company that reviews and evaluates books for Amazon.

Quip Factory
"Five stars (out of Five)

> Quip Factory is a pleasure to peruse, and every page offers another surprising opportunity to manipulate the English Language in new and witty ways. From writers to public speakers to anyone with a passion for Language and a desire to entertain themselves and others, Atwood's book is a must have." – ForeWord Clarion Reviews

"Millions" in the title may have turned some people off when even a "mere" three million would have required an average 10,000 quips per page. That, no doubt, sounded bizarre, but it wasn't because the English language is far more flexible than most people realize. To put "millions" into perspective, two words, can be arranged two ways: three can be arranged six ways – 123, 132, 231, 213, 312 or 321. Whenever an additional word is added, it multiplies the number of arrangements by its amount so, for example, a fourth word would create 24 arrangements (4 x 6) and a fifth 120 (5 x 24). This process is referred to mathematically as "factorial" and is expressed with a number followed by an exclamation. Three factorial is expressed as 3!, four factorial as 4! and so on. Examples:

# of words	# of ways these words can be arranged
5!	120
10!	4,233,600
15!	16,761,821,056,000
20!	695,148,711,762,112,000 – (i.e. quadrillions)

According to Giles Brandreth's marvelous *The Joy of Lex*, most of us have vocabularies in the 20,000 to 30,000 words range. To my knowledge, a word has yet to be coined to describe 20,000! The largest descriptive number in Wikipedia is "vigintillion" – a number followed by sixty-three zeroes—but that is not even remotely close to 20,000! Let's assume for sake of discussion that 20,000! is one giga-vigintillion – 1 GV. That's one billion vigintillions and may seem extreme, but it isn't. Add but one additional word and the total soars to 20,001 GV. Add another and it soars to 400,060,002 GV (20,002 x 20,001 GV). Add another and the total skyrockets to over 80 billion GVs. Add two and the total explodes to over 1.7 trillion GVs. Accordingly, even a miniscule percentage of word combinations is ample to create billions of quips.

Since authoring the *Quip Factory* quips have continue to materialize in virtual tidal waves. When they totaled multi-billions, writing *Quip Thesaurus* became virtually mandatory. That turned out to be fortuitous because, in the process, it became obvious how Quip Thesaurus Appendixes can be used as a **robust resource for writers when "good enough, isn't."** We'll get to that in chapter 12.

A problem with quips is that, when one surfaces, it soon gets overused to the point where it becomes a triple Van Winkle snore inducing cliché a la

throw under the bus
or
lipstick on a pig

Avoiding this, enhancing, enlivening, energizing, and sometimes "envenoming" communication, constantly requires new material. This *Quip Thesaurus*, successor to the *Quip Factory,* contains billions and explains how you can create billions more on your own. Don't fret. If anyone had told me this before I got immersed in quips, I would have referred them to guys who carry coats with long sleeves that tie behind a person's back.

WARNING re: QUIPS

Weird works, silly sells, zany zings, corny, crazy and outrageous can be contagious so proceed with caution if you're worried about of being vilified for having a sense of humor.

CHAPTER I
ANATOMY OF QUIPS

Quip: clever, curious, droll, eccentric, funny, odd, pointed, sarcastic, taunting or witty characterizations, observations, remarks, replies, responses or verbal thrusts that amuse, tease, taunt, surprise, shock denigrate, enrage or eviscerate.

Quips are responses, reactions, replies or rebuttals of people, policies, plans, perceptions, ideas, opinions, organizations, movements, legislation or anything else believed to be harmful, idiotic, inane, insane, adverse, perverse or worse. Quips are usually critical, but that does not prevent anyone from expressing a positive opinion. All that is necessary is to quip its' antithesis. For example, a "gun grabber" (also an opinion), can express that by quipping the NRA.

Quips can range from docile to hostile. A docile example concludes this poem.

> She's glistening waves caressing a moonlit shore,
> a mysterious universe man has yet to explore,
> breathtaking beauty, ecstasy's face,
> a paragon of poise, style, culture and grace.
>
> She's a dancer by Degas, an etude by Chopin,
> a waterscape by Monet, a sculpture by Rodin.
> She's stars gently twinkling on a clear winter night,
> music brought to life, an inspiring sight.
>
> She's Milton's paradise, Shakespeare's reverie,
> a Puccini aria, a Beethoven symphony.
> She's the shimmering sunrise that vanquishes night,
> but other than that she seems all right.

When it comes to hostile quips, it's hard to beat one by William Dean Howells, poet, author and critic, in a letter to Mark Twain in which he referred to one of Twain's employees as

a quadrilateral, astronomical, incandescent SOB.

Quite often a single quip can range from docile to hostile depending upon its audience.

If it weren't for TSA, some people wouldn't have any sex life at all.

This might make airline passengers laugh (or groan), and possibly TSA employees as well, if said in jest, but surely not if said sarcastically by someone who hates TSA and believe its' objective is to condition citizens to being tightly controlled.

Incongruity

Incongruity is the heart of quips and, for that matter, jokes. The difference between the two is that the objective of jokes is to get laughs while the objective of quips is to express opinions and, most often, also to get laughs by characterizing things, people or opinions as silly, insane, inane, obscene, profane, adverse, perverse, weird or worse. Sometimes quips are both funny and disgusting.

> Syria: Country where U.S. is risking world war and blowing billions to help two of our enemies defeat one of our enemies.

There's no better way to put people or things down than to get other people laughing or groaning at them.

Premises and contrasts

Quips consist of **premises** and **contrasts**. Premises are setups for expressing opinions. Examples:

- **Raising taxes in a depression**
- **Trying to spend your way out of debt**

Incongruities are expressed in contrasts that hammer down whatever opinion is being expressed. Examples:

- **is like trying to cure gangrene with a guillotine.**
- **is like trying to fight a forest fire with napalm.**

Note that each of these contrasts work with either of these premises. Often enormous numbers of contrasts will work with a single premise.

Occasionally it is not necessary to state premises because they become evident from contrasts. An attorney friend, Jim Karger, came up a great example. He envisioned a bank offering new customers "**either a toaster or a Nobel Peace Prize**" and followed that with "**Unfortunately, they were out of toasters.**" That was a post-graduate skewering sans a clearly stated premise.

Incidentally, while quips can be laudatory, you won't find many here because dingers, zingers, stingers and barbs are usually far more effective than puffery.

In essence, most quips are analogies. Unfortunately, scores of analogies like:

- **different as apples and oranges**
- **higher than a kite**
- **quick as a wink**
- **smooth as silk**
- **white as snow**

and expressions like:

- **beat around the bush**
- **chew the fat**
- **gild the lily**
- **happy as a pig in slop**
- **kick the bucket**

- **low hanging fruit**
- **run the gamut**
- **shoot the bull**
- **spill the beans**
- **walk the talk**

are used so frequently and routinely they have become clichés or, as Oliver Wendell Holms who coined the word described it, verbicide – "words used so often and indiscriminately that they have lost their cutting edge." Consequently, whether described as verbicide or clichés, they do little to enhance or enliven conversation, oration or written communication. Quips that amuse, tease, taunt, surprise, shock, denigrate, enrage or even eviscerate, usually do.

Elements of quips

There are three elements to quips. One is essential – **incongruity**. It's variously defined as combinations, comparisons or contrasts that may be atrocious, bizarre, conflicting, crazy, discrepant, farcical, foolish, grotesque, inane, laughable, offbeat, preposterous, queer, ridiculous, strange, wacky, weird or worse. We'll discuss the other elements that contribute mightily to the effectiveness of quips – **rhyme** and **alliteration** – in the next chapter.

Naked quips

Most quips are not alliterative and do not rhyme. We'll be referring to them as "**naked quips**."

Formulas

All quips can be reduced to formulas that, in turn, can be used to produce other quips. Some can produce surprising results. We'll discuss one in the next chapter that can produce literally hundreds of millions. If you think that sounds about as likely as finding a 200% off sale at a liquor store, wait until you find out how many hundreds of millions you'll learn how to create.

Our focus

As previously mentioned, premises are whoever or whatever you are skewering so selecting them is, of course, up to you

CHAPTER II
GLORIA STEINEMS

In 1976, Gloria Steinam, a leader of the then nascent women's lib (men are oppressors) movement, delivered a classic quip that was quoted extensively in the media then and is still being mentioned decades later (*Guilty* by Ann Coulter in 2009 and NPR without attribution in 2013):

A woman needs a man like a fish needs a bicycle.

Ms. Steinam's quip can be formulated as

A needs B like X needs Y

with "**A needs B**" being its *premise* and "**X needs Y**" being its *contrast*. Hereafter **X**'s in contrasts will often be referred to as "**pegs**" and **Y**'s as "**pivots**." Accordingly, the peg in Ms. Steinam's analogy is "fish" and the pivot is "bicycle."

Now let's turn to how this formula can be adapted to create additional quips, starting with the proposition that

animals are God's gift to quips

Our opinions of animals vary substantially and we're predisposed to like or dislike them accordingly. If we're looking for sympathy, we can get it with references to kittens, puppies, doves, fawns, etc. If we prefer the opposite, anacondas, cockroaches, mosquitoes, rattlesnakes, sharks, spiders, etc., are locks to work for us.

With human aberrations excepted, animal needs are very basic – accommodating environments, affection, companionship, oxygen, security, sex, water and suitable food. There are many things animals might *like,* such as

Crackerjacks	Oreos
Éclairs	Pancakes
Eggrolls	Popsicles
Fudge	Waffles

but there is little else they actually *need* (i.e. that they cannot live without). That includes most objects, professionals and ailments. Consequently, when juxtaposing the verb "need" with animals as pegs and objects, etc. as pivots, incongruity is certain to surface. See for yourself by contrasting each of the pegs with each of the pivots in Exhibit 1. Afterward make a similar list using whatever animals and objects you choose and you'll get similar results.

Exhibit 1.

A woman needs a man like

Alligators	need	Bagpipes
Bedbugs		Banjos
Caribou	"	Barstools
Donkeys		Bayonets
Eagles	"	Bobby socks
Egrets	"	Eggbeaters
Elephants		Encyclopedias
Falcons	"	Fog horns
Fer-de-lances		Frisbees
Foxes	"	Galoshes
Grizzly bears		Hula hoops
Hamsters		Incinerators
Jackals		Javelins
Jackrabbits		Jockeys
Koalas		Kayaks
Lake trout		Kazoos
Mules		Lifejackets
Octopuses		Masks
Peregrines		Napalm
Polar bears		Oars
Quarter horses		Parachutes
Raccoons		Potty chairs
Rhinos		Propellers
Sloths		Roller skates
Vultures		Tattoos
Walleyes		Thunder mugs
Whippoorwills		Volvos
Wolverines		Waterbeds
Yaks		Yoyos
Zebras		Xylophones

Does an alligator *need* bagpipes, a banjo, bayonet – or any of the other pivots in this exhibit?

6

Obviously not. The contrasts in this exhibit work because they are delightfully incongruous in and of themselves. Can you imagine peregrines needing propellers, rhinos roller skating, zebras playing xylophones?

Now try the same drill contrasting each of the other animals with each of the objects. Is there any combination that doesn't range from incongruous to bizarre? That doesn't mean they're all really great quips but you'll then have 900 from which to choose (i.e. 30 animals that do not need any of the 30 objects) so you should have many viable alternatives.

Pegs and pivots in Exhibit 1 are drawn from Appendix A that lists 2,500 pivots and 730 pegs that do not *need* any of them – i.e. 1,875,000 incongruities.

Alliteration and rhyme are the music of language

At the risk of making Edgar Allan Poe groan in his grave . . . *The Raven* – "Once upon a midnight dreary, while I pondered weak and weary" etc. – published in 1845, is arguably the most prominent poem of all time. Yet, stripped of rhyme and alliteration, it would have survived forever and evermore, as little more, than a famously forgettable rant by a man perturbed by what he thought was a bird.

The *Raven* is compelling evidence that alliteration and rhyme make impressions and have staying power. Accordingly, they are most likely to make the most effective quips.

Alliteration

Pegs and pivots are juxtaposed alphabetically in Appendix A to facilitate creating alliterative quips. Examples:

A woman needs a man like:

- Beavers need buzz saws
- Hamsters need hula hoops
- Jellyfish need jockeys
- Kittens need kazoos
- Otters need oars

Alliteration is the reason why saying someone has "**bats, bees, bugs or butterflies in his belfry**" works far better than saying, for example, that someone has **tsetse flies in his belfry** – even though that would be equally incongruous. Actually, almost any contrast, no matter how bizarre, works if it's alliterative. To illustrate, here's a take on deader than a doornail.

Deader than a:

- dagger
- daiquiri
- decoy
- deutschemark
- diaper
- dinghy
- dipstick
- dirigible
- dumpster
- dunce cap

These pivots are just a few among dozens starting with "d" in appendix A. While on the subject of alliteration, any of the pivots starting with the letter "f" in Appendix A, would have been as effective, or even more effective, than Ms. Steinam's "bicycle." Examples:

A woman needs a man like a fish needs a:

- face lift
- factory
- fedora
- fiddle
- fig leaf
- flugelhorn
- flute
- fly rod
- fly swatter
- fog horn
- footbridge
- footlocker
- footstool
- fork truck
- freezer

- filleting knife
- fire truck
- flame thrower
- flashlight
- football
- fox hole
- Frisbee
- frying pan
- freight train
- funnel
- furnace
- furrier

The point here is that finding contrasts comparable to Ms. Steinam's is relatively easy. Her analogy worked spectacularly because its premise, **a woman needs a man** was so shocking at the time. Still, her contrast – "a fish needs a bicycle" – had a bit of a drawback. Selecting an animal for a peg is usually effective, but in Ms. Steinam's case using "fish" as a peg laid a hard broiled egg. Why? Contrasting women with fish doesn't rate very high on the slick stick.

My dear, you look lovely tonight, as pretty as a fish.

Guys, try that line on your wife or girl friend and five I get your yen she'll "caress" you – with a frying pan. Many other animal alternatives also have drawbacks –

My dear, you look lovely tonight, as pretty as a/an

- ape
- buzzard
- crocodile
- fer-de-lance
- hippo

- pig
- piranha
- rattlesnake
- shark
- tarantula

Run for it Romeo!

Gals, equating your husbands or boyfriends to a fish or numerous other animals would be like baiting a mouse trap with an anaconda – no offence intended for PETA (People for the Ethical Treatment of Anacondas), not to be confused with PETI (People for the Ethical Treatment of Insects), pronounced "petty."

Dear, you're gorgeous, as attractive as a

- haddock
- halibut
- hammerhead
- hedgehog
- heifer

- hippo
- hog
- hoot owl
- humpback
- hyena

So much for sexual warfare.

All the 900 contrasts in Exhibit 1 are incongruous and therefore quippable. Some are uninspiring, but with so many to choose from odds are great that some, and perhaps many, will work quite well. Check with Appendix A and you will find prodigiously more arranged alphabetically to facilitate creating alliterative quips. Following is an excerpt and a few quips drawn from it.

Gamecock, Gander, Gar, Garter snake, Gar fish, Gator, Gazelle, Gecko, Gerbil, German Shepherd, Giant Panda, Giant Squid, Gila monster, Giraffe, Glassfish, Glowworm, Gnat, Gnu, Goat, Golden eagle, Golden retriever, Golden trout, Goldfinch, Goldfish, Goose, Gopher, Gorilla, Gosling, Grackle, Gallows, Gallstone, Galoshes, Gangrene, Gangplank, Garage sale, Garret, Garter, Garter belt, Gas, Gasmask, Gasoline, Gatling gun, Gavel, Gazebo, Geiger counter, Geyser, Gig, Gin, Gin rummy, Girdle, Glacier, Glider, Global warming, Glockenspiel, Glove, Goatee, Go cart, Goggles, Gold,

Grasshopper, Grey fox, Greyhound, Grey wolf, Great Dane, Great white shark, Green snake, Green turtle, Grizzly bear, Groundhog, Ground squirrel, Grouper, Grouse, Guide dog, Guinea hen, Guinea pig, Guppy, Gull, Gypsy moth.

Golf clubs, Gondola, Gown, Grandstand, Grenade, Grill, Grog, Guacamole, Guillotine, Guitar, Gumdrops, Gun, Gunboat, Gutter, Gymnasium, Gyroscope

Like a gander, gar, guppy, etc. needs a:

- girdle
- glockenspiel
- goggles
- gunboat
- grenade

In this excerpt there are 51 pegs and 67 pivots that start with the letter "g." That's 3,417 contrasts. Some other letters produce more. Pegs and pivots for the letter "S," for instance, produce 23,954 contrasts – 118 pegs and 203 pivots.

Rhyme

Appendix B facilitates finding rhyming contrasts. Following is an excerpt followed by a few quips drawn from it.

Bee   BB, bumblebee, artillery, bikini, biscotti, bootee, breeze, BVD, Calliope, CD, Chablis, chamois, Chianti, chickadee, chili, chimpanzee, Chinese, Christmas tree, church key, college degree, daiquiri, DDT, disease, dungaree, epee, factory, Ferrari, flea, fleur-de-lis, Frisbee, goatee, golf tee, grease monkey, greens fee, hemlock tree, hibachi, honeybee, humvee, husky, iced tea, jamboree, Japanese, killer bee, kiwi, law degree, lingerie, LSD, machete, maitre d', manatee, martini, monkey, pass key, pedigree, privy, referee, renminbi, rotisserie, rupee, Sake, settee, shoe tree, skeleton key, snow ski, spaghetti, spree, squeegee, TB, tepee, TNT, tree, trapeze

A woman needs a man like Bees need:

- artillery
- bikinis
- booties
- calliopes
- BVDs

A few more follow.

A woman needs a man like a:

- Bedbug needs a thunder mug
- Caribou needs a tattoo
- Dalmatian needs sex education
- (an) Egret needs a bayonet
- Grizzly bear needs a potty chair

- Hen needs a fox den
- Macaw needs a rickshaw
- Mule needs a barstool
- Mustang needs a boomerang
- Ocelot needs buckshot

- Pike needs a trail bike
- Porcupine needs moonshine
- Reindeer needs a spear
- Shrimp needs a blimp
- Stork needs a pitchfork

With appendices A and B, creating alliterative or rhyming quips should be **easier than finding hay in a needle stack.**

In the next chapter we'll discuss how Ms. Steinem's "original" formula can be adapted to produce phenomenally more contrasts.

CHAPTER III
STEINAM ADAPTATIONS

Old time comedian Joey Adams once opined that there is no such thing as a new joke – only old jokes in new settings with new characters – in other words, adaptations of old jokes. That's not particularly restrictive because it is easy to adapt jokes – as in the following definitions:

Misbehave	Daughter or Mr. Behave
Misdemeanor	Daughter of Mr. Demeanor
Misfortune	Daughter of Mr. Fortune
Mismanage	Daughter of Mr. Manage

There are dozens of other words starting with "mis" that will also work like these. There are even versions for married people – Mrs. Sippi, hit mister and Mr. Fortune's wife misses Miss Fortune.

Following are two descriptions that may qualify as either jokes or quips depending upon whether or not they're targeted at specific individuals.

Married female assassin	Hit Maam
Single female assassin	Hit Miss

Quips as well as jokes are usually highly adaptable and, as you will soon see, sometimes single quips can be adapted to produce billions more.

The difference between jokes and quips is that while the objective of jokes is to get laughs, the objective of quips is, most often, to express opinions that upset, irritate or inspire people to think, act or react. Examples:

Bribe	Political perk
Gun laws	Protection for gangsters and governments
Infinity[2]	Projected U.S. National Debt
FOX on the run	Democrats favorite song
Millions	Fines banksters and other politically connected criminals occasionally must pay for stealing billions
Privacy	Former U.S. constitutional right
Rare	Politicians who have not "accumulated" millions since being elected
Socialism	Fair and equitable distribution of poverty

| Tattoo | Unemployment assurance (Cosby) |
| War | Lifeblood of Military-Industrial complex |

Both jokes and quips are usually funny if people do not feel they are the butt of them. Insofar as these examples are concerned, it wouldn't be wise to expect politicians, the gun confiscation gang, the Fed, soldiers or criminals with tattoos to find them funny. Of course, some quips are so critical that even those who agree with them are unlikely to find them funny. Anti-abortionists, for instance, are likely to agree in principle with a quip like "Right to Choose is an assumed name for the right to kill crowd," but few are likely to find it funny. Likewise, even if modified to "Right to Choose after 20 weeks," it is still not exactly a knee-slapper.

As previously mentioned, if you favor someone or something, you can express that by quipping those opposed to it, but rather than quip, these days most in the public eye, at least, seem to or vilify opponents or ideas they disagree with as harebrained, daffy, idiotic, Neanderthal, uncooperative, pig headed, etc. Anyone can criticize someone or something that way, but it's far more effective to Quip that person or opinion. Example: Wouldn't (what someone proposed, for example) be kind of like feeding foxes to . . . . chickens?

Unimaginative and bland criticism may be newsworthy if made by someone notable and highly regarded. Otherwise it just comes across as mean spirited or dim-witted.

Incongruity is the heart of quips and incongruity is ubiquitous so literally billions of quips can be created with Ms. Steimem's formula. "Billions" probably sounds nuttier than parachutes that open on contact, so let's run some numbers. There are 730 pegs in and 2,500 pivots in Appendix A that can be substituted for pegs and pivots in Ms. Steinem's formula. Collectively they can create 1,825,000 quips – (730 pegs times 2,500 pivots). Thereafter, every time a verb is substituted for "need," it increases the number of quips that can be created with Ms. Steinem's formula by 1,825,000.

Following are 74 such verbs that can increase the total number of Steinem quips to 136,875,000 (75 x 1,825,000).

Accumulate	Covet	Extol	Marvel at	Revere
Ache for	Crave	Fancy	Miss	Savor
Adore	Cuddle	Fondle	Nurture	Search for
Amass	Deify	Gravitate to	Pamper	Seek
Applaud	Delight	Guard	Praise	Stockpile
Appreciate	Demand	Hail	Prize	Swear by
Believe in	Depend on	Haunt	Promote	Thrill
Care for	Deserve	Hunger for	Protect	Treasure
Caress	Desire	Idolize	Ravish	Value
Cater to	Dig	Laud	Regale	Want

Cherish	Dote on	Like	Relish	Weep for
Cling to	Dream about	Lionize	Rely on	Welcome
Coddle	Embrace	Long for	Require	Worship
Collect	Esteem	Love	Respect	Yearn for
Confide in	Exalt	Luxuriate in	Revel in	

Let's look at a few of these.

Women ache for men like apes, abalone, alligators, anacondas, etc., ache for:

- antifreeze
- anchors
- armor
- artillery
- axes

Women believe in men like baboons, bass, beavers, broncos, bunnies, etc., believe in:

- bagpipes
- banjos
- bazookas
- bloomers
- boomerangs

Women cherish men like calves, camels, canaries, chinchillas, etc., cherish:

- calliopes
- cannonballs
- castanets
- cattle prods
- chopsticks

These contrasts are alliterative. That's highly beneficial, but not essential as evidenced by Ms. Steinem's enormously successful "**like a fish needs a bicycle**" contrast. Examples:

Women covet men like baboons, bass, beavers, broncos, bunnies, etc., covet:

- galoshes
- hula hoops
- igloos
- jackhammers
- kung fu

Women cherish men like calves, camels, canaries, chinchillas, etc., cherish:

- leotards
- miniskirts
- napalm
- oboes
- pantaloons

The purpose of quips is to express opinions and everyone has them by the bulging bucket. Ask anyone about virtually anything and odds are they'll have opinions about it. Most of their opinions are likely to be innocuous and unworthy of quipping, but people are a lock to at least have a few dozen of quip-worthy opinions. This is notable because it only takes 8 to produce over a billion quips (8 x 136,875,000 = 1,095,000,000) and, in case you're counting, 731 to produce over a trillion.

You may not have 731 quip-worthy opinions at the moment, but you are likely to have far more than you realize. You can get at least a rough idea of how many by checking the following individuals or issues to determine whether or not you find them worthy of quipping.

Abortion	Drugs	Hunting	President Obama
Any athlete	Economy	Immigration	Profanity
Any bank	Education	Inflation	QE
Any car	Edward Snowden	Internet	Republicans
Any corporation	Egypt	Iran	Ron Paul
Any sport	Environment	Iraq	Rush Limbaugh
Any State	European Union	IRS	Russia
Bailing out banks	Exec compensation	Israel	Soccer
Ben Bernanke	Fast and furious	Lotteries	Stock market
Big Pharma	Food	Mayor Bloomberg	Supreme Court
Bill O'Reilly	Foreign aid	Media bias	Syria
Bradley Manning	Foreign policy	Military	Tattoos
Bribery	Fox News	Minimum wage	Tea Party
Chicago	Free markets	Music	Texas
China	Eric Holder	NAFTA	The environment
Coal	Gambling	Nancy Pelosi	U.S. Constitution
Cost of living	Gov. job report	National debt	U.S. Government
Current events	Gov. COL statistics.	NRA	Unemployment
Death penalty	Greece	NSA	Unions
Deficit spending	Gun control	Obamacare	Vegetarianism

Democrats	Harry Reid	Outsourcing jobs	Vladimir Putin
Detroit	Hillary Clinton	Politics	Weapons
Drones	Homeland Security	Population	Weather

Presumably this resolves concerns about your being able to create billions of quips with this thesaurus. Incidentally, we're about to explore other prolific quip generating formulas, but before getting to them, let's explore four other ways Ms. Steinem's quip can be adapted.

1. Reversing pivots and pegs

Woman (verb) men like pivots (same verb) pegs

This usually works with the following verbs:

- addle
- arouse
- attract
- calm
- cheer

- comfort
- compliment
- conceal
- defend
- delight

- dignify
- elate
- electrify
- enchant
- enliven

- entertain
- enthrall

- fascinate
- fear
- flatter
- frighten
- gratify

- hook
- inspire
- intimidate
- intrigue
- motivate

- need
- oppress
- pacify
- pamper
- placate

- quiet
- reassure

- regale
- relax
- require
- revere
- reward

- romance
- satisfy
- save
- soothe
- spoil

- stimulate
- strengthen
- tempt
- thrill
- titillate

- tranquilize

Examples:

Women addle, arouse, attract, etc., men like:

- Antarctica (verb) Alligators
- Bikinis (verb) Butterflies
- Chopsticks (verb) Sharks
- Diapers (verb) Dingoes
- Hip boots (verb) Hippos

- Pogo sticks (verb) kangaroos
- Saddles (verb) Seahorses
- Saunas (verb) Iguanas
- Stilts (verb) Giraffes
- Submarines (verb) Sardines

2. Peg and pivot reversals with verb substitutions

This involves switching pegs and pivots and then substituting verbs like the following fifty for "need" in Ms. Steinem's formula.

appeal to	charm	dignify	intrigue	reward
appease	chauffeur	elate	juggle	satisfy
arouse	cheer	electrify	lure	save
attract	cling to	enchant	mollify	scare
battle	combat	enliven	motivate	solace
becalm	comfort	entertain	oppress	soothe
bedazzle	compliment	enthrall	pacify	spoil
befuddle	conceal	fascinate	pamper	stimulate
beguile	console	fear	placate	Stir
betray	control	flatter	quiet	Strengthen
bother	corral	frighten	reassure	tantalize
brutalize	cultivate	gratify	regale	tempt
bully	dazzle	hook	relax	thrill
calm	defend	inspire	require	titillate
captivate	delight	intimidate	revere	tranquilize

Examples:

- Women arouse men like bicycles arouse buzzards
- Women becalm men like bazookas becalm butterflies
- Women comfort women like jackhammers comfort jackrabbits
- Women delight men like dynamite delights deer
- Women enchant men like frying pans enchant fish

- Women fascinate men like football fascinates pigs
- Women mollify men like diapers mollify ducks.
- Women placate men like cummerbunds placate polliwogs
- Women solace men like pogo sticks solace kangaroos
- Women titillate men like tuxedos titillate tarantulas

3. Men and Women Reversals

Anyone who disagrees with Ms. Steinem's "woman needs man" quip, can reverse it simply by switching "man" and "woman" in her premise. Then all the man-skewering quips skewer women instead. Examples:

Men need (adore, covet, require, worship, etc.) women like:

- fire ants need, etc., flugelhorns
- hornets need hip flasks
- jellyfish need jockeys
- king snakes need crowns
- penguins need propellers

Men aching for women is like:

- fawns aching for facelifts
- lobsters aching for leotards
- parrots aching for pesticide
- turtles aching for tachometers
- Snails aching for speedometers

Men needing women is like a:

- bunnies needing babushkas
- centipedes needing crutches
- kittens needing cowbells
- rabbits needing Viagra
- sharks needing orthodontists

4. Grafittos

A wag pen-named "Grafitto" came up with an amusing alternative – A man without a woman is like a neck without a pain. That's easy to adapt.

A man without a woman is like a peg without a pivot

Pegs and pivots in Appendix A will all work with this. You can also freelance and toss in any city, company, machinery, music, professional, publication, store or web site, just to name a few options. Obviously these will all work with Steinems – A woman without a man premise.

You can also get animals into the Grafitto act:

A man without a woman is like prey without predators

These options can be doubled by reversing pegs and pivots

A woman needs a man like pivots need pegs

Do bicycles need fish, saddles need seahorses, hip boots need hippos? Crazy stuff, but it's likely to work.

Creating new pegs and pivots

If you like you can increase the number of Steinem quips substantially. All that's necessary is to add pegs and/or pivots. Adding a single peg increases the total by 187,500 (1 peg x 2,500 pivots x 75 verbs). Adding a single pivot will increase your total by 54,700 (730 pegs x 75 verbs). It's quite easy to add pegs in particular. They abound. Just look around. Animals need basics – oxygen, water, security, suitable food, sex, companionship and a favorable environment. Everything else is a potential pivot. Look, for instance, at cars and you'll find potential pivots like:

antifreeze	CDs	gas tanks	jumper cables	rearview mirrors
ashtrays	cigarette	glove boxes	license plates	spare tires
brakes	lighters	GPS	locks	tail lights
bucket seats	cruise controls	headlights	parking lights	tire irons
bumpers	exhaust pipes	horns	power windows	transmissions
carburetors	floor mats	jacks	radios	windshields

Animals do not need any of these and adding each will increase your total by 54,700 because none appear as pivots herein. Look around wherever you go and odds are you'll be able to find many more.

Spare Steinem Contrasts

Following are additional contrasts that might come in handy on occasion.

Like:

- a brain-draining diatribe
- a bull needs a toreador.
- a dentist needs a Rototiller
- a fish (or other aquatic animal) needs a raincoat, umbrella, water wings
- a giraffe needs a ladder, Limbo

- a hippo needs a hula hoop
- a leopard needs spot remover
- a mudpuppy/elephant/ etc./ needs earmuffs
- a peregrine needs a tailwind
- a politician needs a polygraph

- a puma, panda, pollywog, etc., [any animal except a pig works with this] need a pigsty
- a refreshing drink of Drano.
- a sloth needs brakes, a speedometer, track shoes
- a sloth needs Prozac
- a termite needs a taillight

- adopting your grandmother
- amputating the wrong leg
- an arsonist being inducted into the Hall of Flame
- arm-wrestling an ape
- buttering toast with an axe. (Martin Armstrong)

- contending that nothing recedes like success (Wes Pruden)
- criminals need penitentiaries
- deer, ducks or doves need hunters
- fending off a fer-de-lance with a flyswatter
- flying first crass

- forests need chainsaws
- geese need enemas
- graveyards need maternity wards
- handcuffing an octopus
- having a low tolerance for TNT?

- like a Texan getting a "Dear neighbor" letter from New York
- Molotov drain cleaner.
- noggin-knocking nonsense
- Saudis need more sand
- search lights need dimmers.

- the devil needs an ice pick.
- the Joneses trying to keep up with themselves.
- the odds of a pig having a pet python
- thumbs need hammers
- wealthy need welfare

Miscellaneous Pegs and Pivots

Almost all incongruities can be quipped with Steinems. All it takes is pro or con reactions to laws, movements, organizations or subjects like:

Abortion	Firearm confiscation	Spying on citizens
Deficit spending	Fox News	Supreme court
Drones	Legalizing marijuana	U.S. constitution
Drudge Report	NRA	Unions
Fast and Furious	QE	Zerohedge.com

Individuals can also be easily quipped. We'll discuss that in chapter X – Zingers.

CHAPTER IV
ANIMALS AS PEGS AND PIVOTS

So far we've focused upon animals (pegs) and objects (pivots). Now let's see what we can do using animals as both pegs and pivots in the Steinem formula.

Women need, adore, cherish, covet, love, pamper, praise, worship, etc., men like
prey need, adore, cherish, covet, love, pamper, praise, worship, etc. predators

This quip can be adapted prodigiously because virtually every animal has predators and many have substantial numbers of them. For example, the million insects so far identified must have incalculable numbers among 25,000 species of fish, 10,000 species of birds, 4,000 species of frogs, 4,800 species of lizards, 2,900 species of snakes, 400 breeds of chickens, 270 species of turtles and even the 23 species of foxes that eat insects.

Some people already eat insects and there has been talk of late about using insects to provide protein for humans in impoverished areas. It will be devilishly depressing if it comes to that, but great for quipsters:

As appetizing, delicious, delightful, pleasing, palatable, tasty, tempting, etc. as:

- barbecued bedbugs
- bumblebee bread
- creamed cockroaches
- fire ant fudge
- mint-flavored fleas
- mosquito meringue pie
- scalloped scorpions
- toasted tarantula
- wine country cockroach

Consequently, while it's possible to create untold millions of quips with this formula, that's not practical because with the exception of entomologists, ichthyologists, ornithologists, herpetologists and other polyologists, frightfully few people would recognize the vast majority of insects, birds, fish, snakes, etc., so they aren't likely to produce suitable quips.

Let's proceed on the conservative assumption that most people will recognize only the 730 in Appendix A. If each averaged only 10 predators, 7,300 quips could be created using the verb "need." Of course, as previously mentioned 74 other verbs can be substituted for "need" to produce 547,500 more quips.

In sum, with animals as both prey and predators our quip potential soars.

Women pamper men like predators pamper prey

This also works when verbs like those that follow are substituted for "pamper."

Adore	Comfort	Eschew	Kowtow to	Rebuke
Accommodate	Console	Flee	Liberate	Regale
Amuse	Consort with	Flirt with	Loathe	Rejoice
Assuage	Court	Flout	Miss	Repudiate
Becalm	Cuddle	Fondle	Mollify	Repulse
Befriend	Defend	Frolic with	Neglect	Rescue
Beguile	Deify	Gratify	Nourish	Resist
Bemuse	Deplore	Guard	Nurture	Romanticize
Benefit	Despise	Hate	Nuzzle	Satisfy
Boycott	Detest	Help	Obey	Shield
Calm	Disparage	Humor	Oblige	Snuggle
Captivate	Edify	Ignore	Patronize	Soothe
Caress	Elate	Impress	Pet	Spare
Chaperone	Entertain	Infatuate	Placate	Spurn
Charm	Enthrall	Ingratiate	Please	Tickle
Coddle	Enthuse	Jettison	Protect	Weep for

Women protect men like prey protect predators

Dozens of verbs can be substituted for "protect" and produce quips.

Abduct	Coddle	Frighten	Punish
Abuse	Consort with	Guard	Ravage
Accost	Corral	Harass	Rescue
Adopt	Court	Hobnob with	Revere
Applaud	Cuddle	Hunt	Seek
Apprehend	Defend	Imperil	Stampede
Befriend	Deify	Intimidate	Tame
Bludgeon	Devour	Kowtow to	Taunt
Bully	Devout	Lament	Trap
Captivate	Dine with	Love	Tutor
Capture	Elope with	Nuzzle	Value
Caress	Endanger	Overpower	Venerate
Carouse with	Entertain	Praise	Welcome
Chaperone	Escort	Prey upon	Woo
Chase	Flirt with	Protect	

Now let's reverse women and men once again:

Men (verb) women like predators (same verb) prey

Abandon	Comfort	Inspire	Please
Abhor	Dazzle	Invigorate	Preserve
Accommodate	Defend	Jettison	Protect
Aid	Dine with	Liberate	Rehabilitate
Amuse	Feed	Lionize	Sedate
Assuage	Flirt with	Mentor	Spoil
Becalm	Fondle	Mollify	Spurn
Befriend	Guard	Mollycoddle	Tantalize
Beguile	Guide	Pacify	Titillate
Bemuse	Humor	Pamper	Warn
Chauffeur	Inconvenience	Pester	Weep for
Coddle	Indulge	Placate	

Quip options abound when contrasting prey and predators.

Like:

Prey inviting predators to dine
Trying to sell predators to prey
Hiring predators to protect prey
Prey herding predators
Predators protecting prey

Prey preying on predators
Buying predators for prey
Prey need predators
Prey harassing predators
Prey deserve predators

Obviously, names of animals can be substituted for "prey" and "predator" so these formulas can produce prodigious numbers of additional quips.

CHAPTER V
JOHNNY CARSONS

Harking back to *The Tonight Show* with Johnny Carson, when a word like "attractive," "busy," "easy," "happy," etc., would come up in conversation, his sidekick Ed McMann, and the audience, would chime in enthusiastically with "How attractive was she?" "How busy was he?" "How happy was she?" "How easy was it?" Carson would respond with quips like:

- **As attractive as a bull moose in a bikini.**
- **As busy as a lifeguard in a car wash.**
- **As happy as a pig in a pizza parlor.**
- **As easy as juggling jellyfish.**

The formula for this **As X as Y** has probably been used since people lived in caves, but we're blaming it on Carson because he's somewhat better known than the average Precambrian cave quipster and, unlike Carson, there's no evidence that Precambrian cave quipsters continued to repeat punch lines until their audiences finally gave up and laughed.

For openers, all Steinem pegs and pivots can be adapted to Carsons using the following formula.

As (adjective) as a peg is with a pivot.

As happy, etc., as a:

- baboon with a banjo
- cockatoo with a catamaran
- giraffe with stilts
- peregrine with a parachute
- seahorse with a saddle
  etc.

Each adjective used in this formula produces 1,875,000 quips (i.e. one for each of the 730 pegs multiplied by the 2,500 pivots). Inasmuch as there are hundreds, if not thousands, of adjectives among over 5,000 in Appendix E that may be used with this formula, brain-numbing numbers of quips can be created with it. All that's necessary is to contrast them with the opposite of what they describe – large with small, fast with slow, strong with weak, exciting with dull, happy with sad, easy with hard, etc. Sumo wrestler–jockey examples:

- As effective, popular, exciting, etc., as a Sumo wrestler moonlighting as a jockey
- As victorious, successful, imposing, etc., as a jockey moonlighting as a Sumo wrestler.
- As likely, certain, brilliant, unbelievable, etc., as a Sumo Wrestler winning a marathon.
- As common as Sumo marathons.
- As inconceivable, rare, happy, thrilling, unbelievable, etc., as a jockey winning a slam-dunk contest.

In the examples that follow many other adjectives may be substituted for those used.

As:

- agile as a bull-legged bronco.
- ambidextrous as an anaconda.
- American as borscht, chop suey, wiener schnitzel.
- bald as a peeled onion.
- cheap as cab fare to Cairo.

- common as sunshine in coal mines.
- compatible as lions and lamb chops.
- competitive as a water polo team with drowned horses.
- credible as a 400 pound diet book author.
- credible as a cockroach is edible.

- religious as an agnostic praying mantis.
- crooked as a barrel of snakes. (Byron King)
- dangerous as dueling with butter knives.
- dangerous, deadly, etc., as a man-eating amoeba, butterfly
- deceptive as a cross-eyed ping pong player.

- delicious as Drano.
- difficult as eating éclairs.
- difficult as getting your name on a mailing list.
- divisive as a guillotine.
- dumb as robbing tourists returning from Las Vegas.

- easy as amputating a wooden leg.
- easy as falling asleep in class.
- easy as selling teleprompters in D.C.
- easy as taming tarantulas.
- easy as threading a sewing machine – while it's running.

- elusive as a greased eel.
- ethical as a Christian holding four aces. (Mark Twain)
- exciting as driving square gold balls.
- flattering as a self-portrait that looks like a donkey.
- grand as quicksand.

- handicapped as a golfer playing with his boss.
- happy as a heard of hopped-up hippos.
- happy as a mosquito in a nudist colony.
- happy as hens in fox dens.
- hard as enduring a sibling's prosperity.

- hard as underestimating the honesty of politicians.
- hard as finding salt in seawater.
- haughty as a guppy named Goliath.
- honest as the day is wrong.
- hot as Juneau in January.

- inevitable as debt and taxes.
- intelligent as a tree full of owls. (Wes Pruden)
- likely as an heiress getting divorced.
- likely as Picassos needing spray paint.
- mature as making up ones' mind with marijuana.

- menacing as a bull-legged butterfly, flea with fangs, cowardly kitten, etc.
- modest as a first string king.
- much panache as a cache of cash.
- overbearing as politicians who believe everything they say.
- often as giraffes need garter belts, stilts, galoshes, girdles, gin, gangrene, etc.

- plausible catching salmon with soup.
- popular as lickerish pizza.
- practical as giving bald men hair spray.
- prestigious as having a reserved seat on an electric chair.
- productive as paper-training a goose.

- proud as a plucked peacock.
- proud as a snail arrested for speeding.
- quiet as a riot.
- reticent as rabbits on Viagra.
- safe as a man-eating elephant.

- sensible as trying to sell bacon to pigs.
- sexy as a topless tarantula.
- skinny as a skeleton.
- snore inducing as campaign speeches.
- studious as a fifth year freshman.

- subtle as the "b" in subtle.
- surprising as a happy marriage. (Oscar Wilde)
- thoughtful as wishing someone a happy first marriage.
- tipsy as a tight tight end.
- challenging as hunting in a zoo.

- unfortunate as backing into an uninsured tree.
- unfortunate as getting sick on a day off.
- warm as a sarongs in Antarctica.

We've discussed how different adjectives can be coupled with events to produce quips. Now let's look at a few examples of how individual adjectives can be used to create multiple quips.

As agile as:

- a fly with one wing.
- beavers in ballet slippers.
- butterflies in blizzards.
- oiled otters.
- manatees on water skis.

- payloads in hearses.
- quail in gales.
- sea snakes in snowstorms.

As attractive as:

- 20 muscle frowns.
- bouquets of used sneakers. (P.J. O'Rourke)
- condors in pinafores.
- iridescent pheasants.
- the person we see in the mirror. (Ambrose Bierce)

- the south end of a horse going north. (Coleman Brown)
- whitewall tires on garbage trucks.

As brave as:

- baboons with blow torches.
- soldiers with yellow hearts.
- stingray's fiancées.
- wolverines on Dexedrine.

As broke as:

- boxers who can't whip cream.
- Mercedes mechanics in Podunk.
- pickpockets in nudist colonies.

As busy as:

- Botox salesmen in Burbank.
- cops in doughnut shops.
- Gucci salesmen in Dogpatch.
- pace cars at snail races.
- sardines on caffeine.

As careful as:

- kangaroos on pogo sticks.
- nudists in cactus patches.
- porcupines making love.
- woodpeckers in petrified forests.

As clever as:

- drinking instant coffee to save time.
- feeding the hand that bites you.
- the guy who invented burlap underwear.
- the genius who invented color radio.

As comfortable as:

- Eskimos in kimonos
- long tailed cats in rooms full of rocking chairs. (Tennessee Ernie Ford)
- starlings in snake pits.
- vultures on valium.

As common as:

- alligators in Antarctica.
- asps in Alaska.
- bald men fighting over combs.
- balloons at porcupine parties.
- barbershops with emergency rooms.

- broad waists and narrow minds.
- centerfolds in church bulletins.
- condors in pinafores.
- dead-end one-way streets.
- fairy Godfathers

- honest burglars.
- giraffes in Greenland.
- ice fishing in the Sahara.
- little league polo.
- Maalox on tap.

- mice in snake pits.
- pet wolverines.
- second skydiving accidents.
- soup kitchens in the Hamptons.

As convincing as:

- Adam telling Eve "It's not mine."
- bald barbers promoting hair restoration.
- Noah predicting drought.

As crazy as:

- getting your tongue notarized so people will believe what you say.
- having pets vacation with taxidermists.
- raising apes in apiaries.
- seeking shelter from tornados in outhouses.
- selling cows to buy milk. (Peter D. Schiff)

As dumb as:

- complaining when crude floods your salt mine.
- gargling with a revolver.

- kissing porcupines.
- marrying a self-made widow.

As easy as:

- amputating the wrong leg.
- catching butterflies in a hurricane.
- cherishing humility – in others.
- counting raindrops in the Amazon.
- enduring adversity – in others. (Mark Twain)

- finding out a woman's age by asking her sister-in-law.
- gaining weight on a diet.
- giving centipedes pedicures.
- incubating eggs in microwaves.
- killing bedbugs with bazookas.

- losing weight taking a bath.
- playing spin the gin – bottle.
- selling parachutes with money back guarantees.
- shutting a mouth with a foot in it.
- Dribbling a shot-put

As effective as:

- circular firing squads.
- getting the last word in first.
- giving others the benefit of your inexperience.
- sterilizing storks to control population.
- wake-up calls at Forest Lawn. (Joey Adams)

As enjoyable as:

- enforced fasts.
- being popular – in Podunk.
- cicada serenades.
- feeding doves – to Dobermans. (National Lampoon)
- pulling your own teeth.

- root canals.
- trips through sewers in glass bottom boats.

As entertaining as:

- golf on radio.
- income tax audits.
- sail races.
- water skiing in the Sahara.

As exciting as:

- centipede stampedes.
- eluding jealous husbands – when you're 90.
- gutter balls.
- one game winning streaks.

As fast as:

- building inspectors in nudist colonies.
- galloping glaciers.
- quail in a gale.
- souped-up sloths.

As fearsome as:

- agitated amoebas.
- designated drunk drivers.
- one-armed octopuses with arthritis.
- Tootsie Roll famines.

As happy as:

- a mule in a car pool.
- cats in mouse houses.
- doctors operating on malpractice attorneys.
- glass salesmen after riots.
- grizzlies in salmon runs.

- hypochondriacs who are actually sick.
- kangaroos on pogo sticks.
- lawyers with new suits.
- rabbits in snake pits.
- undertakers at celebrity funerals.

As helpful as:

- doctors with their own cemeteries.
- giving others the benefit of your inexperience.
- napalm in fighting fires.
- seeking shelter from tornados in outhouses.

As important as:

- hindsight when women buy slacks.
- peeling watermelons.
- reductions in farce.
- welfare for the wealthy.

As likely as:

- bears needing BVDs, beanies, bazookas, boomerangs, buckshot, butchers, barstools, butcher knives
- guys whistling at women's brains.
- eagles teaching penguins to swim.
- glacier forming global warming.
- Heaven needing fire trucks.

- Rockafellers applying for welfare.
- seahorses needing saddles, shot puts, safety belts, sarongs, shotguns, skillets, sledgehammers, etc.
- sloths being arrested for speeding.
- the Pope subscribing to Playboy.
- throwing a dinner – and missing.

- hippos needing hot pants, hooch, Harleys, harpsichords, hand grenades, etc.
- politicians reading the constitution.

As lively as:

- centipede stampedes.
- macho mummies.
- payloads in hearses.

As menacing as:

- boxers who can't whip cream.
- docile doves.

- game hens in fox dens.
- poison ivy in nudist colonies.
- rickshaws at Daytona.
- wolverines on Dexedrine.

As novel as:

- 95 year olds plagued with peer pressure.
- abortion clinics with two year waiting lists.
- bald barbers promoting hair restoration.
- Noah predicting rain.
- second skydiving accidents.
- tattooed prudes.
- taxis driven by American citizens. (Steve Allen)

As popular as:

- alcoholics synonymous.
- alligator hunting in Antarctica.
- doctors who keep stethoscopes in freezers.
- dress poker in nudist colonies.
- kissing porcupines.

- little league polo.
- mountain climbing in Iowa.
- people who know how to play bagpipes but don't.
- shutting a mouth with a foot in it.
- silicone salesmen at beauty contests.

- the person we see in the mirror. (Ambrose Bierce)
- water skiing in the Sahara.

As profitable as:

- 100% off sales.
- Nieman-Marcus stores in Zimbabwe.
- selling hotdogs in Hades.
- selling snow shovels in summers to avoid competition.

As prosperous as:

- Gucci salesman in Dogpatch.
- Mercedes mechanics in Podunk.
- pineapple farmers on Mt. Everest.

As rare as:

- 20 pound guppies.
- finding clam in clam chowder.
- forgetting your twin's birthday.
- kangaroos playing kazoos.
- married cub scouts.

- reform school scholarships.
- snails leaving vapor trails.
- timid tarantulas.
- vegans applying for hunting licenses.
- virgin widows / widowers.

As relaxed as:

- pit bulls on Prozak.
- rabbits in snake pits.
- vultures on valium.
- wolverines on Dexedrine.

As sexy as:

- a bull moose in a bikini.
- a tomcat in heat.
- having the body of a 30 year old – Ford.

As slick as:

- asking someone where they got their face lift. (P.J. O'Rourke)
- deer guts on a door knob. (Doug Dillard)
- greased eels.
- telling a woman she's younger than she looks.

As tasty as:

- dill pickle popsicles.
- armadillo on the half shell
- hard broiled eggs.
- Kaopectate cocktails.
- Kentucky fried buzzard.

As useful as:

- barstools in whirlpools.
- napalm in forest fires.
- weather vanes in hurricanes.
- wooden legs in forest fires.

As welcome as:

- malpractice attorneys in hospitals.
- icebergs in punchbowls. (Wes Pruden)
- cats in mouse houses.
- foxes in hen houses.
- losing jobs at unemployment offices.

Time to move on to Jay Leno inspired quips.

CHAPTER VI
JAY LENOS

This chapter's name and content derives from Jay Leno's prescient

**Isn't trying to spend your way out of debt kind of like
trying to drink your way out of alcoholism?**

This can be formulated as:

Isn't (premise) kind of like trying to cure (a problem) with (its cause)?

This differs from other formulas we've discussed in that it's in the form of a question so it leaves it up to readers or listeners to decide whether or not they buy into an idea. It's a bit gentler than others because it's not necessary to buy in wholeheartedly, only "kind of." When people do, they have a form of ownership.

All that's necessary to create quips with "Lenos" is to think of a problem and it cause and then insert both in this formula. Examples:

Isn't trying to spend your way out of debt kind of like trying to cure:

- anorexia by dieting?
- bankruptcies with bailouts?
- cancer with cigarettes?
- despotism with fascism?
- favoritism with chauvinism?

- freedom with socialism?
- gangrene with a guillotine?
- inflation with a printing press?
- insecurity with criticism?
- insomnia with coffee?

- Marxism with communism?
- Montezuma's revenge with Ex-Lax.
- obesity with candy?
- Saint Vitus' dance with Dexedrine?
- unemployment with higher taxes?

The Leno formula can be adapted to produce additional quips by varying questions somewhat and substituting verbs.

Varying questions

Aren't the odds of being able to spend your way out of debt kind of like the odds of being able to drink your way out of alcoholism?

Substituting verbs

Another alternative is to substitute other verbs for "curing." Here's the formula for that:

Isn't that kind of like (pegs) needing, etc. (pivots)?

Sound familiar? It should because it hitchhikes on, and works as extensively as, the Steinem "need" formula. And, as was the case with Steinems, creating quips like those that follow is simplified using Appendix A which juxtaposes pegs and pivots alphabetically and Appendix B that lists pegs and pivots that rhyme with them. Examples:

Alliteration

Isn't X kind of like:

- armadillos needing, coveting, worshiping, etc., armor?
- buffalos needing babushkas?
- condors needing catacombs?
- drakes needing decoys?
- emus needing epees?

- giraffes needing glockenspiels?
- hyenas needing hip boots?
- ibex needing icebergs?
- jackals needing jackhammers?
- koalas needing kayaks?

Rhyme

- loons needing, coveting, worshiping, etc., bassoons?
- malamutes needing zoot suits?
- night hawks needing tomahawks?
- ocelots needing yachts?
- peacock needing hemlock?

- quail needing e-mail?
- rhinos needing mistletoe?
- sardines needing slot machines?
- termites needing dynamite?
- unicorns needing flugelhorns?

"Naked"

- alligators needing, etc., bedpans?
- buffalo needing cattle prods?
- centipedes needing pedicures?
- deer needing forest fires?
- eagles needing binoculars?

- geese needing, etc., diapers?
- giraffes needing stilts?
- vultures needing teleprompters?
- walleyes needing zippers?
- zebras needing skating rinks?

Here are illustrations in which other verbs substituted for "needing":

Isn't (premise) kind of like trying to sell:

- anchors to angelfish?
- blimps to buzzards?
- cookbooks to cobras?
- dental floss to ducks?
- elevators to eagles?

- flame throwers to flamingos?
- garters to gophers?
- hooch to hoot owls
- ice picks to iguanas?
- jackhammers to jellyfish?

Isn't (premise) kind of like buying:

- deutschemarks for aardvarks?
- pantaloons for baboons?
- swizzle sticks for chicks?
- boxing gloves for doves?
- glockenspiels for eels?

- underpants for fer-de-lance?
- crowbars for gars?
- crying towels for hoot owls?
- sweaters for Irish Setters?
- javelins for jaguars?

Isn't X kind of like trying to convince:

- alligators to purchase antifreeze?
- bluebirds to purchase balloons?
- cheetahs to purchase cannons?
- dromedaries to purchase Drano?
- egrets to purchase epees?

- ferrets to purchase fiddles?
- groundhogs to purchase golf clubs?
- haddock to purchase harpoons?
- insects to purchase insecticide?
- jaguars to purchase skis?

Isn't X kind of like trying to convince:

- antelopes to buy jump ropes?
- bats to buy coolie hats?
- clams to buy battering rams?
- dolphins to buy violins?
- eels to buy high heels?

- foals to buy totem poles?
- grasshoppers to buy clodhoppers?
- horned toads to buy commodes?
- Ibex to buy Tex-Mex?

Isn't that kind of like saying:

- appaloosas depend upon axes?
- bloodhounds depend upon bagpipes?
- coyotes depend upon casinos?
- Dalmatians depend upon daggers?
- elephants depend upon earmuffs?

- fireflies depend upon Frisbees?
- guinea pigs depend upon grenades?

- hummingbirds depend upon howitzers?
- inchworms depend upon I-pods?
- jackasses depend upon judo?

Isn't that kind of like wearing:

- armor to recycling plants?
- bulletproof vests to kindergarten?
- jewelry to riots?
- pajamas to weddings?
- pork chop underwear into lion dens? (Alonzo Brown)

- safety belts in church?
- snowsuits on safaris?
- sweatpants in saunas?
- tuxedos in junkyards?
- zoot suits at symphonies?

Isn't that kind of like trying to convince, induce, motivate, etc., any animal to drink:

- cognac
- champagne
- moonshine
- sake
- tequila

to drive:

- bulldozers
- dump trucks
- rickshaws
- hearses
- taxis

to play:

- bagpipes
- flugelhorns
- glockenspiels
- piccolos
- xylophones

wear:

- aprons
- bibs
- cummerbunds
- dresses
- evening gowns

Now let's take a ~~goose~~ gander at additional Leno contrasts you may be able to use or adapt:

Isn't that, or wouldn't that, be kind of like:

- a counterfeiter refusing to pay his debts?
- a dog biting a flea?
- a flea winning first prize at a dog show?
- a hayride through Hades?
- a kneeling ovation?

- a shoe company having a centipede as a mascot?
- a teacher playing hooky?
- a topless bomb shelter?
- a will being regarded as a dead giveaway?
- abortion clinics with two year waiting lists?

- adding tenderizer to tequila?
- adopting a grandfather?
- an all-terrain submarine?
- arguing with an asp?
- arm-wrestling with an octopus?

- asking fire hydrants how they feel about dogs?
- bachelors who think one can live as cheaply as two?
- berating college athletes for playing like amateurs?
- blaming rain on people who carry umbrellas? (Peter D. Schiff)
- brides bringing dates to their weddings?

- bungee jumping with a stiff rope?
- buying a dog to hunt fleas?
- buying a harness for a dead horse?
- buying safety shoes for a centipede?
- catching fish so big it isn't necessary to lie about them?

- celebrating an F because it's not an F minus? (Peter D. Schiff)
- chickens coveting Colonel Sanders?
- claiming the government as a dependent at tax time?
- commuting a life sentence to 40 years for a 60 year old?
- comparing oranges and road apples?

- contending that spanking is physical education?
- convicting five suspects because one of them may be guilty?
- cosmic arrogance? (Krauthammer)
- cure meningitis with mercurochrome?
- dancing with a diamondback?

- declaring war by mail?
- designating drunks as drivers?
- digging your way out of a ditch? (Hillary Clinton)
- dining with cannibals?
- disarming an octopus?

- draining an ocean with a thimble? (Senator Charles Grassley)
- drilling a hole in a canoe to let water out?
- drinking instant coffee to save time?
- drop-outs tutoring honor students?
- drowning yourself because you're mad at a lifeguard?

- eating soup with chopsticks?
- eels needing electric shock treatment?
- emergency entrances to beauty parlors? (Phyllis Diller)
- entering a unicycle in the Tour de France.
- falling asleep the minute your feet hit the pillow?

- fighting fire with napalm.
- finding free cheese in mousetraps? (Russian proverb)
- Finding the cure for sobriety, honesty, decency, bravery, intelligence, common sense,
- flunking kindergarten?
- forgetting your twin's birthday?

- getting a new leash on life?
- giving an upper bunk to an elephant?
- giving umbrellas credit for rain?
- giving up your mind for Lent?
- going to an opera to get some sleep?

- going to Heaven without the inconvenience of dying?
- having four kids and one phone?
- having politicians negotiating contracts with the people who bribe them. (Lou Holtz)
- having the face of a Saint – Bernard?
- having a low tolerance for TNT?

- having the life expectancy of a heart donor?
- having a seeing-eye kitten in a kennel.
- heating the houses by burning the furniture? (Ludwig Von Mises)
- hiring Dale Earnhardt to drive a snow plow.
- housebreaking rattlesnakes?

- jacking up a giraffe?
- judging doctors by the praise they get from undertakers?
- Juggling jackhammers?
- juggling jellyfish?
- killing bedbugs with bazookas?

- kleptomaniacs asking what they can take for it?
- lapdogs that won't let you sit on their laps?
- learning to drive by accident?
- love at first feel.
- looking for loopholes in the Constitution?

- looking forward to a tax audit?
- make-up making you look younger than you aren't?
- manicuring ladyfingers?
- microwaving chickens so they'll lay boiled eggs?
- misquoting yourself? (Lyle H. Long)

- mistaking strychnine for quinine?
- mountain climbing in Iowa?
- nudists fighting over three piece suits?
- paint brushes taking credit for Picassos?
- paranoids with real enemies? (Henry Kissinger)

- passive use of polar heat?
- politicians getting three weeks' vacation – monthly?
- proctologists using two fingers to get second opinions?
- prescribing a heart transplant, for a headache?
- putting newspapers under a cuckoo clock?

- putting safety glass on fire alarms?
- quitting a job to prevent being late for work?
- racing a gazelle with one leg tied behind your back?
- raising a whale in an aquarium? (Chris Mayer)
- raising pigs in a penthouse?

- requiring policemen to carry popguns?
- requiring schools to provide sleeping pills?
- requiring sirens and seatbelts on tricycles?
- Russian roulette with six bullets?
- Sampson needing a haircut?

- saying the way to a man's heart is through his socks?
- sedating a sloth?
- selling sarongs in Antarctica?
- selling spot remover to leopards?
- selling hunting licenses in a zoo?

- shooting ducks in buckets?
- shot putting sidearm?
- sky-diving with an umbrella?
- spinning the unspinable? (Steven F. Hayes)
- taking a joy-ride on a landslide?

- taking a raincoat into a shower?
- teaching predators how to defend themselves from their prey?
- the greatest thing since sliced beer.
- the pot calling the kettle "Ma"?
- throwing a shot put sidearm?

- Tiger Woods subscribing to *Golf for Dummies*.
- tipping musicians with food stamps? (Joe Kirkpatrick)`
- topless tarantulas?
- treating college athletes like amateurs?
- treating truth like an abscessed wisdom tooth?

- treating tumors with tourniquets?
- trying to convince Madonna that baseball is our favorite pastime?
- trying to cram a megawatt idea into a squat-watt brain.
- trying to disarm an octopus?
- trying to eat steak with a spoon?

- trying to frighten a fer-de-lance with a flyswatter?
- trying to grow pineapples in Nome?
- trying to handcuff an octopus?
- trying to outlaw snoring?
- trying to plug a volcano? (Jason Hommel)

- trying to provoke a python with a pea shooter?
- trying to raise mice in a snake pit?
- trying to sell fire trucks in heaven?
- trying to sell swords to swordfish?
- trying to shut a mouth with a foot in it? (Gideon Wordz)

- trying to slam a revolving door?
- trying to sleep off insomnia?
- trying to tame inflation by raising taxes?
- turbo charging a tricycle?
- vegans catering barbecues?

- waiting for your ship to come in – in a train station?
- Waterproofing diapers?
- Water-proofing whisky?
- Wearing ear muffs at a opera?
- Wearing high heels to bed?

- worms holding fishing tournaments?
- wrestling a grizzly bear wearing pork chop underwear. (Alonzo Brown)

CHAPTER VII
MARK TWAINS

Mark Twain came up with a great quip about his parents whom he described in his Autobiography as "**not conspicuously honest.**" Following are words that can be substituted for "honest" in his quip.

X is not conspicuously:

Admirable	Credible	Fascinating	Kind-hearted	Revolting
Adorable	Credulous	Fashionable	Knowledgeable	Right-minded
Adroit	Cuddly	Fearless	Laudable	Romantic
Affable	Dashing	Feckless	Law-abiding	Scrupulous
Agreeable	Dazzling	Fetching	Lenient	Seductive
Altruistic	Debonair	Flamboyant	Loveable	Sensible
Amiable	Decent	Forgiving	Loyal	Serene
Amusing	Dependable	Formidable	Magnanimous	Skinny
Angelic	Desirable	Friendly	Magnificent	Smart
Appealing	Dexterous	Frugal	Married	Sober
Appreciative	Diplomatic	Generous	Merciful	Softhearted
Astute	Discreet	Genial	Moderate	Solvent
Awe-inspiring	Distinguished	Gifted	Modest	Speedy
Awesome	Divine	Glamorous	Moral	Spontaneous
Benevolent	Domesticated	Gleeful	Nimble	Spry
Blissful	Down-to-earth	Good-hearted	Noble	Stimulating
Brainy	Educated	Good-humored	Normal	Striking
Brave	Effective	Good-natured	Objective	Strong
Bright	Electrifying	Gorgeous	Open-minded	Stunning
Brilliant	Eloquent	Graceful	Optimistic	Suave
Candid	Empathetic	Gracious	Peaceful	Subtle
Capable	Enchanting	Grateful	Personable	Sweet
Charismatic	Encouraging	Gregarious	Pleasant	Swift
Charitable	Endearing	Guiltless	Poised	Sympathetic
Charming	Engaging	Healthy	Polished	Tactful
Cheerful	Enjoyable	Helpful	Polite	Talented
Cherubic	Enlightened	High-spirited	Pragmatic	Temperate
Chivalrous	Enterprising	Honest	Prescient	Tolerant
Circumspect	Entertaining	Honorable	Presentable	Trusting
Civic-minded	Enthusiastic	Housebroken	Pretty	Trustworthy

Civil	Enviable	Humble	Professional	Unobtrusive
Clean	Esteemed	Humorous	Prolific	Unsullied
Clever	Estimable	Impressive	Prudent	Uplifting
Coherent	Ethical	Industrious	Qualified	Well-adjusted
Comforting	Excellent	Influential	Quick-witted	Well-behaved
Competent	Exciting	Innocent	Radiant	Well-informed
Conscientious	Experienced	Innovative	Rational	Wide-awake
Considerate	Expressive	Inspiring	Reassuring	Witty
Cordial	Extravagant	Intelligent	Refined	Worthwhile
Courageous	Exuberant	Interesting	Reliable	Young
Courteous	Faithful	Intrepid	Respectful	Zealous
Creative	Farsighted	Jovial	Responsible	

Adverbs can often be substituted for "conspicuously."

adamantly	aggressively	perceptibly	fiendishly	rigorously
aggressively	amiable	deliriously	glaringly	robustly
appallingly	certifiably	dependably	impeccably	tediously
astonishingly	compassionately	dreadfully	imperceptibly	terribly
avidly	compulsively	ecstatically	impulsively	tenaciously
abhorrently	conscientiously	endearingly	intolerably	unflappably
abnormally	convincingly	enviably	memorably	unscrupulously
absolutely	crushingly	exceptionally	meticulously	vehemently
absurdly	dangerously	excruciatingly	picturesquely	wondrously
aggravatingly	detectibly	ferociously	reliably	zealously

Surprisingly, perhaps, you can also substitute negative for positive traits. X is not conspicuously dishonest, for example, suggests that X is actually dishonest, but not conspicuously so.

Abhorrent	Bloviated	Daft	Ham-handed	Rapacious
Abnormal	Blundering	Dead	Harebrained	Repulsive
Abominable	Blustery	Deadly	Haughty	Rowdy
Abrasive	Boastful	Deafening	Heinous	Sadistic
Abstinent	Bogus	Deathly	Hypocritical	Sane
Absurd	Boisterous	Debased	Hysterical	Satanic
Abusive	Bombastic	Debauched	Idiotic	Scandalous
Abysmal	Bone-headed	Debilitating	Immoral	Scatterbrained
Adolescent	Bonkers	Decadent	Impolite	Scheming
Aggravating	Boorish		Inane	Schizophrenic

Agitated	Boring	Deceitful	Incompetent	Scurrilous
Agonizing	Brainless	Deceptive	Inconsiderate	Shady
Alarming	Brutish	Decrepit	Ineffective	Shallow
Alienating	Bull-headed	Defamatory	Insane	Sickening
Amoral	Bungling	Defective	Insolent	Sinister
Anemic	Bush-league	Delirious	Intolerable	Sleazy
Angry	Calamitous	Demanding	Irascible	Sloppy
Annoying	Callous	Demeaning	Irascible	Slovenly
Antagonistic	Cantankerous	Demented	Irrational	Sophomoric
Antiquated	Catty	Demoniac	Jaded	Strange
Antisocial	Caustic	Demonic	Juvenile	Stupid
Apathetic	Chaotic	Denigrating	Klutzy	Tawdry
Appalling	Cheap	Deplorable	Kooky	Thievish
Arbitrary	Claustrophobic	Depraved	Lascivious	Toxic
Arrogant	Clownish	Depressed	Laughable	Troublesome
Atrocious	Clueless	Deranged	Lazy	Two-faced
Audacious	Clumsy	Derelict	Lecherous	Tyrannical
Autocratic	Cocky	Derisive	Lethargic	Uncooperative
Avaricious	Conceited	Derogatory	Lewd	Uncouth
Awful	Confined	Desolate	Looney	Undependable
Awkward	Conflicted	Despairing	Loquacious	Undesirable
Banal	Confounding	Despotic	Mangy	Unfair
Barbaric	Confrontational	Devious	Maniacal	Unmerciful
Batty	Conniving	Diabolic	Masochistic	Unpleasant
Bawdy	Contemptible	Diabolical	Mean-spirited	Unpopular
Beastly	Contrary	Dilapidated	Morbid	Unqualified
Bedraggled	Corrigible	Diminished	Nauseating	Unrealistic
Befuddled	Corrosive	Dimwitted	Neurotic	Unreliable
Bellicose	Corrupt	Disagreeable	Notorious	Unscrupulous
Belligerent	Corruptible	Dishonest	Nutty	Unstable
Berserk	Cowardly	Dizzy	Obnoxious	Unwholesome
Bestial	Cranky	Dreadful	Offensive	Vapid
Bigoted	Crazy	Dull	Oppressive	Vindictive
Bitter	Creepy	Eccentric	Outrageous	Vitriolic
Bizarre	Criminal	Evil	Overbearing	Vulgar

Blatant	Crocked	Exasperating	Peculiar	Weird
Bleak	Crotchety	Fiendish	Persnickety	Whacko
Blistering	Crude	Finicky	Petty	Wicked
Bloated	Cruel	Flaky	Pompous	Woozy
Block-headed	Crushing	Flighty	Profane	Worthless
Bloodcurdling	Cuckoo	Foolish	Promiscuous	Wretched
Bloodthirsty	Cursed	Goofy	Quirky	Yellow
Bloody	Cynical	Grotesque	Radical	Zany

CHAPTER VIII
LIPSTICKERS

This chapter's name is derived from a quip that has been thoroughly overworked

Like Putting Lipstick on a Pig.

Heretofore, pegs have been animals and pivots have been objects, but that is reversed with this formula. Here's an illustration.

Like putting lipstick on a / an:

- alligator
- barracuda
- cobra
- donkey
- elephant

- firefly
- guppy
- hamster
- impala
- jackal

Once again, alliteration flourishes with animals whose names start with "l."

Like putting lipstick on a:

- Labrador
- ladybug
- lake trout
- lamb
- lamprey

- lark
- lemming
- lemur
- leopard
- lizard

- llama
- loon

As you've no doubt surmised, there are many alternatives to "lipstick." Following are a few.

Exhibit 2

Like putting:

armor	on	alligators
bibs	"	baboons
corsets	"	chinchillas
diapers	"	ducks
earrings	"	emus
flak jackets	"	fleas
girdles	"	gorillas
helmets	"	huskies
incense	"	iguanas
jockstraps	"	jellyfish
kilts	"	koalas
leotards	"	lobsters
mascara	"	mink
negligees	"	newts
overshoes	"	otters
pinafores	"	pit bulls
roller skates	"	rams
spurs	"	stingrays
tuxedos	"	tadpoles
undies	"	unicorns
veils	"	vultures
wigs	"	walruses
zoot suits	"	zebras

These contrasts are all incongruous, but the best are those that are alliterative – i.e. located across from one another on the same line. This exhibit can be expanded substantially by adding virtually any other animal:

Like putting pinafores on:

- piranhas
- Pekinese
- pelicans
- pythons
- poodles
- pumas

Like putting diapers on:

- Dalmatians
- diamondbacks
- dingoes
- Dobermans
- dolphins
- donkeys

Like putting mascara on:

- mink
- monkeys
- musk ox
- mosquitoes
- mountain goats
- magpies

This list can be expanded even further by employing other objects. Examples:

Like putting:

• aprons	on	alligators
• air bags	"	"
• anchors	"	"
• bikinis	"	baboons.
• bloomers	"	"
• boutonnieres	"	"
• chastity belts	"	chimpanzees
• cologne	"	"
• cummerbunds	"	"

- diapers   "   donkeys
- dunce caps   "   "
- dungarees   "   "

- earmuffs   "   eagles
- earrings   "   "
- evening gowns   "   "

- face paint   "   flamingos
- fedoras   "   "
- flak jackets   "   "

- galoshes   "   gorillas
- girdles   "   "
- goggles   "   "

- hair spray   "   hyenas
- handcuffs   "   "
- high heels   "   "

Appendix A facilitates all this as illustrated with an excerpt from it and a few contrasts that can be produced with it.

Labrador Retriever, Ladybug, Lake Trout, Lamb, Lamprey, Lapdog, Largemouth Bass, Lark, Leech, Leghorn, Lemming, Lemon Shark, Lemon Sole, Lemur, Leopard, Leopard Seal, Lhasa Apso, Lice, Lightning Bug, Ling, Lion, Lion Fish, Lipizzaner, Lizard, Llama, Lobster, Locust, Loggerhead Turtle, Longhorn, Loon, Louse, Love Bird, Lynx

Label, Laboratory, Lace, La cross, Ladder, Ladle, Lamp, Lampshade, Lance, Landfill, Landing Gear, Land Mine, Land Rover, Landslide, Lantern, Lariat, Laryngitis, Laser, Lasso, Latrine, Laughing Gas, Laugh Track, Laundromat, Lavatory, Law Degree, Lawnmower, Laxative, Leash, Leavenworth, Leggings, Lectern, Legerdemain, Lei, Lemonade, Leotards, Leukemia, Levis, Lexus, Librarian, Library, Lie Detector, Lifeboat, Life Insurance, Lifejacket, Life Raft, Lighthouse, Lightning Rod, Limousine, Lingerie, Liposuction, Lipstick, Liquor, Liquor Store, Literature, Lumberjack, Lock, Lockjaw, Locomotive, Logo, Loincloth, Lollypop, Longbow, Long Johns, Loom, Looney Bin, Lottery, Lotto, Luau, Luggage, Luger, Lute, Lyre, Lyricist

Like putting lamp shades, leashes, leotards on:

- Labradors,
- ladybugs
- lake trout
- lambs
- lampreys
  etc.

Now let's look at another – Like putting X on Y – exhibit. It varies from exhibit 2 in that, instead of featuring alliteration, it features rhyme.

Exhibit 3

Like putting:

carburetors	on	alligators
petticoats	"	Billy goats
negligees	"	blue jays
pinafores	"	boars
mistletoe	"	buffalo
tattoos	"	caribous
stiletto heels	"	electric eels
stretch pants	"	fire ants
sugar cane	"	great Danes
boutonnieres	"	grizzly bears
spritz	"	jackrabbits
track shoes	"	kangaroos
mittens	"	kittens
skis	"	manatees
toupees	"	manta rays
coolie hats	"	vampire bats
loincloths	"	sloths
Old Spice	"	mice
Bobby sox	"	musk ox
zoot suits	"	newts
sombreros	"	sparrows
rheostats	"	tomcats

- boxing gloves   "   turtledoves
- veils   "   whales

Appendix B makes it easy to expand this list. Here's another excerpt from it followed by a few illustrations:

Bee   BB, **bumblebee**, artillery, bikini, biscotti, Chablis, chamois, chili, **chimpanzee**, Christmas tree, church key, college degree, daiquiri, DDT, epee, factory, Ferrari, fleur-de-lis, Frisbee, goatee, golf tee, grease monkey, greens fee, hemlock tree, hibachi, **honeybee**, **husky**, iced tea, jamboree, **killer bee**, **kiwi**, law degree, lingerie, LSD, machete, maitre d', **manatee**, martini, pass key, pedigree, privy, referee, renmimbi, rotisserie, Saki, shoe tree, skeleton key, snow ski, spaghetti, squeegee, tepee, TNT, trick knee, water ski

Like putting bikinis, lingerie, skis, etc., on:

- bees
- bumblebees
- chamois
- chickadees
- chimpanzees

- fleas
- honeybees
- huskies
- killer bees
- kiwis

- manatees
- monkeys
- Pekinese
- spider monkeys
- turkeys

Onward . . .

CHAPTER IX
INTERPRETOLOGY

Interpretology is the "science" of deciphering how words may, and often should, be interpreted.

The following interpretations are all incongruous and, as such, are usually quippable in one context or another including, for example.

Term (i.e. "Terp")

Socialism (i.e. fair and equitable distribution of poverty)

These terms and terps will also work with other formulas we've discussed. Examples:

> **Carson: As satisfied as diners who leave 1% tips.**
> **Leno: Wouldn't that be about as popular as a 1% tip?**
> **Steinem: Women praise men like waiters praise 1% tips.**
> **Twain: 1% tips are conspicuous way of expressing opinions.**

Following is a formula that will work with all the terms and "terps" that follow. When perusing them, please remember that, with quips, silly sells, weird works, groans grab, corny, crazy and outrageous can be contagious.

"When X says (term), that usually means ("Terp")

TERM	"TERP"
Amateur	College athlete under assumed name
Ancient	Year old computer
Appropriate	Theft in polite society
Bipartisan	Duplicitous
Bonus	Perk for poor performance
Booze	Cure for sobriety
Brag	Prevaricate
Bribe	Presidential perk
Burlesque	Politics
Burning question	Who will be the happiest politician in hell?

Campaign contribution	Down payment
Cancer cured	Announcement in 1888 AMA Journal (true)
Candid	Insulting
Capital	Seat of misgovernment
Ceasefire	Calm before the norm
Censor	Generate interest
CFTC	Market manipulator facilitator
Citizen	Government ATM
Collaborate	Capitulate
Con	Pro in drag
Confident	Nervous under an assumed name
Consistent	Reliably incompetent
Constitutional	Irrelevant
Corruption	Invitation for whistle blowers
Gun laws	Protection for gangsters and governments
Courageous	Afraid to retreat
Criminal	Profitable
Critic	Commentator with fine toothed axe.
Curfew	Law that prevents kids from acting like adults
Debriefed	Nude
Delegate	Spread blame
Delusional	Bet on nag with 300 pound jockey
Deliberate	Stall / Pretend to decide
Delight	Darken
Denial	Reflexive political response
Detroit	Too broke to bail
Disappoint	Impeach
Discrimination	Substitute for thinking
Dishonest	Wealthy
Driver Education	Learning to drive by accident
Drone	Killing device designed to "save lives"
EEOC indictment	Charging jockey with race discrimination
Economic forecast	Financial guesstimate
ENRONerate	Swindle
Ethical	Undetected

Evil	Root of all money
Exile	Refuge for whistleblowers
Explanation	Alibi
Extinct	Middle class in America.
Extremist	Honest politician
EXXONerated	Pardoned oil company executive
Familiarize	Strip search
Federal Reserve	Body that gives multi-billion bail-ins to banks that own it
Felon	Former Illinois governor
Football coach	Highest paid faculty member
Forbid	Deny others rights you enjoy
Forecast	Premeditated hunch
Fox News	Truth serum for "progressives"
FOX on the run	President Obama's favorite song
Free market	Former market characteristic
Freedom Bell	Symbol of former freedom
Frightened	Cognizant.
Gold	Demonized in U.S., worshiped elsewhere
Golf	Game president Obama would prefer to play eight days a week
Govern	Rule
Gullible	Voter
Hazardous	EPA's synonym for "safe"
Hero	Cornered coward
Hisicane	Male hurricane
Honest	Under observation
Ignoramiable	Ignorant, but nice about it
Immigration	Something American Indians did not need
Immune	Connected in D.C.
Incarcerated	Temporarily unelectable
Inedible	Diet friendly
Intrepid	Clueless
Innocent	Undetected
Irrefutable	Witness free
IRS	Infernal Retribution Service
Low calorie	Tasteless

Lucky	Losing political candidate
Lugubrious	Succinct in DC
Leasing	Alternative when politicians can't be fully afforded
Legal secretary	Girl over 18
Liberal	Unencumbered with reality
Maxiscule	Miniscule unmasked
Menacing	Truthful
Mental kleptomania	Stealing others' ideas (Bucky Fuller)
Minimum wage	Ample for people who don't drive, eat or rent
Miniskirt	Floor length after taxes
Mischievous	Daughter of Mr. Chievious
Modest	Unenlightened
Moonshine	Only untaxed beverage
Murder for hire	Mafia drone profit center
No money down	Booby trap
Noise	Political discourse
Notarize	Attest to misstatement
Notorious	Successful
Nude	Debriefed
Oath	Candor suppressant
Octogenarian	Coming qualification for social security
Optimistic	Delusional
Oratorical	Sleep inducing
Originality	Undetected plagiarism (Ralph Inge)
OSHA rule	Safety glass on fire alarms
Pass	Fail to flunk
Peace	Job killer / nightmare for Military-industrial complex
Pessimist	Realist
Political discourse	Putting mouth where the money is
Politician	Parasite
Politics	Cure for prosperity
Political role model	Charles Ponzi
Premeditated	Poorly planned
Pro	Undetected con
Positive	Slightly less uncertain

Potty chair seatbelt	OSHA requirement
Predictable	Deceased
Post birth abortion	Planned parenthood issue
Popular	Promiscuous
Popularity	Reward for making jerks feel good about themselves
Rationale	Lame excuse
Reliable	Never failing to fail
Right to Life	Assumed name for Right to Kill after 20 weeks crowd
Role models	Assaunge, Snowden, Manning, Ponzi
Researching	Confirming preconceived misconceptions
Reverse engineer	Purloin
Recreate	Plagiarize
Shaking hands	Sex after 70.
Sacrifice	Doing without what others don't have
Sad	Cognizant
Same	Odds of winning lottery whether or not you play (Parker)
Secrecy	Blame in hiding
Secure	Incarcerate
Senate	Inane asylum
Senior citizen	Superannuated adolescent
Solar energy	Perpetual pollution solution
Spanking	Physical education
Sterilize storks	Abortion alternative
Student loan	Path to Hell in a helicopter
Studious	Slow learner
Study	Lowest priority for college students
Stupidious	Convergence of stupid and hideous
Success	Being right half as often as weathermen are wrong
Surgeon	Organ grinder
Surviving	New name for "thriving" in this economy
Tattoo	Unemployment assurance
Taxing taxes	Revenue enhancement suggestion
Tenure	Reward for academic incompetence
Thinking	OK as long as it doesn't become habit-forming
Toast	Wishful drinking

Tolerance	Forgiving those as guilty as we are
Trophy husband	Apparition
Trophy wife	Wealthy widow
Truthful	Alternative-less
TSA agent	Dream job for amateur proctologist
Two-faced	Flexible.
Weaker sex	Intimacy after sixty
Wicked	Prevalent.
Will	Dead giveaway
Wisdom	Archaic attribute
Wise crack	Honest opinion
Wicked	Prevalent

CHAPTER X
ZINGERS

"X' in the quips that follow represent your favorite acting adolescent(s) at any age who you might like to harpoon. They are arranged topically.

Ability

- X couldn't find a cow in a coat closet.
- X couldn't find an elephant in a petting zoo.
- X couldn't make a hyena laugh.
- X couldn't steal second base in the middle of the night.
- X couldn't manage snake control in Ireland.

- X is a one-trick phony.
- X couldn't think with all the noise his butterfly was making.
- X doesn't have lots to be modest about. (Winston Churchill)
- X doesn't let failure go to her head.
- X has no talent, but at least he doesn't brag about it.

- X hasn't a single redeeming defect. (Disraeli)
- X is so old he only chases women downhill.
- X never fails to fail.
- X sounds like Tiny Tim trying to imitate Luciano Pavarotti.

Age

- Odds of X making sense are about the same as odds that cattle will die of old age.
- When X was young the Dead Sea was only sick. (Milton Berle)
- X hopes to live to 100 or eternity, whichever comes first.
- X is at the age where he won't take "yes" for an answer.
- X is the world's oldest adolescent.

- X isn't likely to be attractive until he reaches 40 . . . again.
- X isn't as young as he acts.
- X thanks God that wrinkles don't hurt.

Appearance

- If it weren't for mosquitoes X would never wear clothes.
- The baby looked like X – until turned right side up.

- X buys things he doesn't need to impress people he doesn't like.
- X does a convincing job of imitating a corpse.
- X escaped by the skin on her tooth.

- X has a new hair color – platinum bald.
- X has never needed to wear a disguise at a costume party.
- X is grateful that wrinkles can be cured by taking your glasses off.
- X is in love with being in love – with himself.
- X is irritatingly slender (Myrna Blyth)

- X is not concerned about being bald because he was born that way.
- X is so sick he looks like the picture on his driver's license.
- X is so skinny she could hula hoop a Froot Loop. (Katy Austin)
- X is tall, dark and hysteric.
- X looks like she puts makeup on with boxing gloves.

- X looks like a Saint – Bernard
- X looks well-reared – in front.
- X needs suspenders to hold up his girdle.
- X needs to have his face lifted – with a noose.
- X received second billing in *Beauty and the Beast*.

- X thanks God that wrinkles don't hurt.
- X's clothes fit her like a suntan.
- X's parents should have run away from him.
- X's wife extracted three of his teeth – with her fist.

Arrogance

- If X hadn't been born, he thinks people would wonder why. (H. V. Prochnow)
- X is always letting off self-esteem.
- X never hurts anyone's feelings – unintentionally. (Oliver Hertford)
- X would ask for separate checks at the Last Supper.
- X digs foxholes with nine irons.

- X is like a nudist who can run 100 yards in nothing.
- X is so flexible he can pat himself on the back.
- X is so quick she could thread a sewing machine while it's running.
- X makes a Pit Bull look sedate. (Shannon Thompson)
- X makes a sloth seem as agile as a greased eel.

- X runs like a hippo in hip boots.
- X should yell "Fore" when he putts.
- X uses his shins to find things in the dark.
- You can time X's marathon with a calendar.

Bravery

- Cowards run in X's family.
- Pit Bulls are for wimps. X has a pet bull.
- When X was a kid, he played spin the cop.
- X fights and runs away so he'll live to fight and run another day.
- X is a pants-wetting coward. (Ann Coulter)

- X is as brave as a pregnant pole vaulter.
- X is as brave as the first person who ate an oyster
- X is as gutless as a skeleton
- X only hits babies in self-defense.

Credibility

- Automatic toilets flush when X walks by.
- Of his own free will, X has remained 35 for years. (Oscar Wilde)
- Only half the lies X tells are premeditated.
- The only time X says "yes" is if asked if he's straight or gay.
- The only way anyone would believe X is if he admitted being stupid (etc.).

- There is no evidence that X has ever done anything intelligent.
- Truth flies south when X opens his mouth.
- X abuses the privilege of being stupid.
- X can cure you no matter how well you are.
- X can't be wrong all the time, but he certainly seems to try

- X can't even be right more often than the weatherman is wrong.
- X has not exactly been gagged by reality.
- X is a world-famous ignoramus.
- X is much older than his twin sister.
- X knows everything about nothing.

- X needn't fear being believed.
- X only gets things right by accident.
- X won the Helen Keller award for far-sightedness. (James Dines)

Beverages

- X contends that he's sober, but isn't likely to need embalming when he dies.
- X has found the cure for sobriety.
- X is a recovering Teetotaler.
- X is not inconvenienced by being sober.
- X is suffering from bottle fatigue.

- X isn't likely to need embalming when he dies.
- X's morning after lasts all day.

Criticism

- X has a lot of nerve making fun of an ostrich.
- X has a right to his stupid opinions
- X is a fault-finder with a built in magnifying glass.
- X is a misfortune teller.
- X would criticize crabs for not walking straight.

Decisiveness

- With X it's donkey see, donkey do.
- X once came dangerously close to making a decision.
- X's indecision is final.

Egotism

- X thinks the world of his wife's husband.
- If (verb that follows) could cure disease X would deserve a Nobel Prize.

Belittling	Boasting	Conniving	Prevaricating	Ridiculing
Bellyaching	Bragging	Defrauding	procrastinating	Waffling
Blaming	Cheating	Demonizing	Provoking	Wishing
Blundering	Complaining	Maligning	Ranting	

- X cherishes humility – in others.
- X has everything he deserves but an inferiority complex.
- X has hallucinations of grandeur.
- X is always me-deep in conversation.
- X wallows in self-adulation.

- X needs to straighten his halo. (Rich Galen)
- X suffers from self-inflation.

- X thinks the Jones are trying to keep up with him.
- X will never be accused of having an inferiority complex.
- X will plead guilty for the honor of being accused.

- X's head is too big for his toupee.

Faith

- God proved he had a sense of humor when he created X.
- How in Hades could X ever get to heaven.
- X feels as if he's gone to heaven without the inconvenience of dying.
- X is looking for a loophole in the ten commandments.
- X thanks God he is an atheist.
- X would rate the second coming 3.2 on a scale of 1 to 10. (Bruce D. Wood)

Happiness

- When X grows up he wants to be a little boy. (Joseph Heller)
- X is happily married, but his wife isn't
- X is living high on the frog.
- X is not happy, but he is not unhappy about it. (Alan Bennet)
- X is unhappy about going without things the Rockefellers have.

Health

- X couldn't pass a drug test if he studied for it.
- X feels bad because he doesn't feel worse.
- X has invented a new drug that cures Viagra.
- X could get blood poisoning from biting his tongue.
- X isn't fat, he's just gravity friendly

- X's medicine had foam on it.
- X would ask for a second opinion if he passed a physical

Honesty

- Even Ripley couldn't believe X.
- I couldn't tell the truth if his coffee was laced with sodium pentothal.
- If X is not lying, he's taking obscene liberties with the truth.
- Is theft the key to X's success?
- It's a good thing X wasn't under oath when he said that.

- Lie-detectors short circuit when X enters their room.
- People would only believe X is if he admitted he was dishonest, lying, stupid, etc.
- Sometimes X comes perilously close to telling the truth, being honest, etc.
- The only reason X ever tells the truth is because he has a bad memory.
- There is always the haunting possibility that X is telling the truth.

- What X doesn't know about law would fill a prison cell.
- Why pick on X? He hasn't swindled anyone in days.
- X belongs in the Prevaricator Hall of Fame.
- X dishonestly cannot remember.
- X has been found insubordinate for telling the truth.

- X is an honorary member of the Crook of the Month club.
- X is doing his best to prove that P.T. Barnum was right
- X is not inconvenienced by being honest. (Twain)
- X is so poor he doesn't even have to cheat on his income tax.
- X obviously hasn't been chugging truth serum.

- X only has three shoplifting days before Christmas.
- X only tells the truth because it's easier than memorizing. (Krauthammer)
- X opposes bribery, theft, etc., but he's not a fanatic about it.
- X remembers honesty – barely.
- X told the truth once and has never forgiven himself.

- X will double-cross that bridge when he comes to it.
- X's logic, competence, honesty, etc., is underwhelming
- X's word is as good as a laxative.

Ignorance

- Even X's wisdom tooth isn't all that bright.
- If X could profit from his mistakes he'd be a millionaire.
- If X were twice as bright, he'd still be dim.
- Mind readers should only charge X half price.
- Only a pig considers X an equal. (Churchill)

- The second dumbest guy in the world should be grateful for X.
- What X doesn't know about law would fill a prison cell.
- X always fails to miss the point. (Lyle H. Long)
- X always recognizes mistakes the fifth time he makes them.
- X can't even remember what he meant to forget.

- X cannot leave bad enough alone.
- X doesn't let common sense interfere with his better judgment.
- X gave up thinking for Lent.
- X has a clinker in his thinker.
- X has never been able to abstain from idiocy,

- X has reached rock bottom, but continues to dig.
- X is 100% right – 2% of the time.
- X is a member of MENSA in absentia.
- X is a neophyte's neophyte.
- X is a self-made idiot.

- X is as behind time as the back of a clock.
- X is mentally unemployed. (Oscar Wilde)
- X is tenaciously ignorant. (Matt LaBash
- X is unencumbered with common sense
- X isn't sure if Mickey Mouse is a cat or a dog.

- X knows everything about nothing.
- X once came dangerously close to making sense.
- X should be playing pin the tail on himself. (Dennis Miller).
- X thinks a vegetarian is a horse doctor.
- X thinks drill sergeants are dentists.

- X was the only one in his kindergarten older than the teacher.
- X's brain is on an extended vacation.
- X's common sense is in solitary.
- X's ignorance is encyclopedic.
- X's word is like a laxative.

- X would take soap to a bridal shower.

Language

- When X talks there isn't a dry seat in the audience
- X is inebriated with the exuberance of his own verbosity. (Disraeli)
- X is so verbose he can bring tears to glass eyes.
- X runs out of ideas before he runs out of words.
- X speaks English like a native – Ethiopian

- X suffers from a lack of laryngitis.
- X talked so loud he woke up his audience.
- X went on vacation and hasn't been obscene since.
- X would have to clean up his language to go to a stag party.

Marriage

- If X weren't married, he'd be his own worst enemy.
- The biggest mistake X ever made was saying "I do."
- X doesn't know if he can make his wife happy because he's never tried.
- X flips spouses like steal estate agents flip houses.
- X has a low tolerance for marriage.

- X has been faithful to his wife dozens of times.
- X remembers sex
- X thinks there's no hell because he's always been a bachelor.
- X was a pallbearer at his wife's wedding.

Money

- A fool and X's money are soon partners.
- If X really doesn't need something, sometimes he won't buy it.
- If X wrote a dime novel, it would be over-priced
- When X discovered the key to financial success they changed the lock.
- X aspires to be as rich as someone who doesn't pay taxes.

- X has the first dollar he ever made – but nothing else.
- X is going to run away from home as soon as he can afford one.
- X started at the bottom and stayed there.
- X will help you pick your own pocket.

Personality

- Acid wouldn't melt in X's mouth. (Joey Adams)
- Machiavelli would have loved X.
- People often have a paralyzing suspicion that X is trying to be funny, etc.
- People would call X an "ass" if it wouldn't upset PETA.
- Too bad X isn't housebroken.

- Unfortunately, X can't help being X.
- X has a weird sense of rumor.
- X has found the cure for popularity.

- X is a part-time human being.
- X is a perpetual emotion machine.

- X is a veritable ulcer farm.
- X is as nervous as a mailman at a dog show.
- X is bound to be the most popular, respected, deserving, etc., person in Hades.
- X is eminently dislikeable
- X is perfectly willing to let others have his way.

- X is reliably unreliable.
- X is so fastidious he washes the soap after he takes a bath.
- X is unpredictable – one never knows how wrong he is going to be.
- X won an Academy Bored award.
- X would complain of the noise if Michael Jordon, Oprah or Mother Teresa knocked.

- X has never been burdened with:

Ambition	Courage	Enthusiasm	Impartiality	Success
Brains	Creativity	Fairness	Kindness	Tact
Bravery	Decency	Friendliness	Modesty	Tolerance
Charm	Dependability	Honesty	Reliability	Virtue
Compassion	Ethics	Humility	Sanity	Wisdom

- X suffers momentary lapses into:

Coherency	Credibility	Honesty	Loyalty	Reliability
Competence	Decency	Humility	Normalcy	Sanity
Congruency	Fairness	Kindliness		

Politics

- Most people wouldn't vote for X for all the gold-plated tungsten in Fort Knox.
- There aren't enough diapers in (name state or town) to absorb X's campaign promises.
- X ran unopposed and came in third.

Sex

- X collects old masters and young mistresses.
- X fired his secretary for a mistake she wouldn't make
- X has a 36 bust and a matching IQ.
- X is as sexy as a topless tarantula.
- X knew here before she became a virgin. (Oscar Levant)
- X pulled a bloomer. (Joey Adams)

Sobriety

- To X a day without wine is like a night without moonshine.
- With X it's wine, women and so-long.
- X can't be a heavy drinker because he only weighs 115 pounds.

- X covets Beethoven's Fifth.
- X doesn't drink any more – or less.
- X drinks to forget he drinks. (Joe E. Lewis)
- X graduated Magma Cum Loaded.
- X has a severe case of bottle fatigue.

- X isn't as loaded as other people look.
- X must have been wearing a lampshade when he said that.
- X opens conversations with a cork screw.
- X suffers from liquor mortis.
- X was so high he could hunt ducks with a rake. (Tony Ullrich)

Talk

- If there's something to be said about X he's usually saying it.
- If X keeps swearing someone is going to make a soprano out of him.
- If X said what he thought he'd be popular in Leavenworth.
- Some tell you everything they know – X tells you more.
- X always has the last word – and all those preceding it.

- X can compress the most words into the smallest idea of anyone. (Abe Lincoln)
- X can't even keep his mouth shut when he's listening.
- X has a great sense of rumor.
- X has never missed a good opportunity to keep his mouth shut.
- X is not addicted to understatement.

- X isn't lying, he just has trouble telling the truth. (Britt Hume)
- X needs a mud flap on his mouth
- X never catches fish as big as his stories.
- X never seems to know when to say nothing.
- X should take his clodhoppers off before he puts his foot in his mouth.

Tolerance

- X has a low tolerance for tolerance.
- X forgives his enemies – after their funerals.
- X came out and admitted he's not gay.

Miscellaneous

- If X tried to shoot himself, he'd miss.
- In nursery school, X majored in marijuana.
- We elected the enemy and he is X. (Dr. Seusse)
- X faithfully ignores the Constitution, Federal law, and common sense.
- X flunked spelling in school, but he's great on Twitter.

- X is an avid reader of *Poor Housekeeping*.
- X is as welcome as a baby before a wedding.
- X is so lazy it takes him eleven hours to get eight hours sleep.
- X ran over a truck.
- X survived potty training – barely

- X threw a fit clear to Mars.
- X's popularity has exploded by centimeters.

CHAPTER XI
QUIP SELECTION SUGGESTIONS

If someone or some entity does or says something you deem decidedly worthy of infamy, like for instance, someone in congress saying "We really need to vote for (a bill) to find out what is in it," there are several ways you can quip it.

Steinems: "We (citizens, taxpayers, etc., need that like kittens need cancer" (or any other Steinem contrast)

Carsons: "That makes almost as much sense as fighting fire with kerosene" (or something else incredibly stupid).

Lenos: "Wouldn't that be kind of like trying to find the cure for sobriety?"

Twains: "Regrettably, that not a conspicuously sane thing to say."

You can also borrow an incredibly versatile quip from Former Senator Zell Miller that works universally. "If X would say that in the country, it would really help the crops."

Any are likely to work, but one is likely to work best so it is advisable to consider alternatives before deciding which to use.

Some quips are so inherently incongruous (polite term for brain staining, idiotic, goofy, inane, insane, adverse, perverse, adverse, or worse) that they work remarkably well on their own.

In the course of your decision making process, remember that alliteration and rhyme are the music of language and fashion your quips accordingly so your opinions will be most likely to make impressions and be repeated. This Thesarus is structured to facilitate creating alliterative and rhyming quips. The 730 pegs in Appendix A work alliteratively with any of its' 2,500 pivots, but most effectively when pegs and pivots are alliterative (i.e. start with the same letter) or rhyme with each other. Appendix B facilitates creating quips that rhyme by listing all pegs with pivots that rhyme with them. Examples:

Like pigs need:

peashooters	periscopes	pickup trucks	plows	pontoons
pedometers	petticoats	pistols	pogo sticks	potty seats
penitentiaries	pianos	pitchforks	playpens	prison

Like bees need:

bikinis	church keys	Ferraris	Humvees	shoe trees
bootees	daiquiris	Frisbees	machetes	squeegees
calliopes	DDT	hibachis	pedigrees	trapezes

To illustrate, wouldn't Ms. Steinem's "like a fish needs a bicycle" have been more effective with either pivots starting with "f" as previously mentioned or pivots starting with "p"?

Incidentally, while alliteration and rhyme tend to make impressions with staying power, quips also get such results. An excellent example of this is a letter I received from an old (take that both ways) friend many of you may remember from his movies or, most likely his role as anchorman on the Murphy Brown television series. Following is his response to a quip laden note I sent in celebration of his 77th birthday.

CHARLES KIMBROUGH

In case you haven't found Kimbrough's letter readily decipherable here are its' key elements.

> "It's wonderful, I hope you haven't copyrighted it! Even if you have, it's too late. I've told it to Beth (his wife, aka "Vera" on Alice TV show), to my son (John Kimbrough, head of rock band Walt Mink), and I hope to tell everyone I know."

I didn't make a copy of my note to Kimbrough but as best I can recall, it said something about his reaching the stage of his advanced adolescence where it is socially acceptable to be too lazy to loaf and something about him feeling like he's gone to heaven without the inconvenience of dying. Nonetheless, whatever the quip(s) were, I wish I had mentioned they were from this Quip Thesaurus.

In sum, when deciding upon quip, it's advisable to focus first on finding alliteration and rhyme.

Quip Crib Sheets

Have you ever been confronted with something really bizarre, but unable to come up with a suitable quip in response in a timely manner? If so, you might want to consider keeping a quip crib sheet on hand for quick reference. Steinem's, Carsons and Lenos are all excellent sources to draw from because they all can be adapted to respond to virtually anything people say or do.

Furthermore, if you're going to a meeting of some sort and know what subjects are likely to be discussed, you might want to consider preparing responsive quips in advance and cribbing them.

CHAPTER XII
WHEN GOOD ENOUGH ISN'T

"Good enough" is usually OK for casual or informal communication, but is likely to reflect poorly on writers of articles, books or speeches when better, possibly even perfect words, are available.

Writers and speakers are blessed with resources to facilitate rising above "good enough " – regular and rhyming dictionaries, thesauruses and the internet among them, but there has not been a convenient resource to facilitate incorporating alliteration. Obviously all alliterative words are in dictionaries, but wading through tens of thousands of definitions in tiny type to find the best alliterative alternatives can be a tedious, tiresome and time-consuming task. That is unfortunate because

alliteration and rhyme are the music of language.

The purpose here is to provide a convenient vehicle to facilitate alliteration. In essence, it is a definition-free dictionary with lists of adjectives, adverbs and verbs. They're listed alphabetically because alliterative words most often start with the same letter.

> ➤ **B**aboons need **B**azookas, **B**agpipes, **B**abushkas, **B**anjos, **B**loomers
> ➤ **D**ucks need **D**iapers, **D**ecoys, **D**entures, **D**ynamite, **D**iving boards
> ➤ **H**ippos need **H**ip boots, **H**elicopters, **H**ammocks, **H**arpoons, **H**ighchairs

Occasionally, words that start with different letters also work alliteratively. Examples:

C & K – **C**ats, **C**amels, **C**aribou, etc., need **K**ayaks, **K**ilts, **K**azoos, etc.
C & Q – **C**ougars, **C**ockatoos, **C**ows, etc., Covet **Q**uicksand, **Q**-tips, **Q**uagmires, etc.
F & P – **F**errets, **F**leas, **F**awns, etc., fancy **P**hones, **P**heasants, **P**hotography, etc.

Consequently, when looking for alliterative words starting with any of these you may be able to find viable alternatives among these combinations.

Plus

Even when alliteration is not an issue, Appendix A that follows is a convenient resource for finding the most appropriate words to express yourself or confirming that those you already have in mind are the clearest and most effective – i.e. better than "good enough." Accordingly, the "right" word under a given set of circumstances is most often a word that is alliterative or rhymes – as illustrated in Appendix B.

APPENDIX A
ALLITERATION OPTIONS

Aardvark, Abalone, Afghan Hound, Airedale, Akita, Albacore, Albatross, Alley Cat, Alligator, Alligator Gar, Alligator Lizard, Alpaca, Amoeba, Anaconda, Anchovy, Angelfish, Angleworm, Angora Cat, Angora Goat, Ant, Anteater, Antelope, Ape, Appaloosa, Arabian Horse, Arctic Fox, Armadillo, Asp, Ass, Atlantic Salmon

Abacus, Accelerator, Accident, Accordion, Accountant, Acne, Acrobat, Adhesive Tape, Aerobics, Agony, Airbag, Airbrakes, Airbus, Airfare, Airmail, Airport, Air Rifle, AK47, Alarm Clock, Algebra, Alibi, Alimony, Allowance, Almanac, Alphabet, Altimeter, Ambulance, Ambush, American Express, Ammunition, Amnesia, Amtrak, Amusement Park, Anchor, Anorexia, Antennae, Antifreeze, Anvil, Aphrodisiac, Apron, Aria, Arthritis, Aquaplane, Area Code, Arena, Aria, Ark, Armada, Armament, Armchair Armoire, Armor, Army, Arrow, Arsenal, Arsenic, Art Deco, Arthritis, Artillery, Asbestos, Astronomy, Astroturf, Athletes Foot, Atlas, ATM, Attaché case, Attic, Attorney, Audi, Auto, Autobahn, Autopsy, Avalanche, Aviator, Axe, Axle

Baboon, Badger, Bald Eagle, Baltimore Oriole, Bantam Rooster, Barnacle, Barn Owl, Barracuda, Bass, Basset Hound, Bat, Beagle, Bear, Beaver, Bedbug, Bee, Beetle, Beluga Whale, Bengal Tiger, Bighorn, Billy Goat, Bird, Bird Dog, Bird of Paradise, Black Bird, Black Drum, Black Lab, Black Mamba, Black Squirrel, Black Vulture, Black Widow Spider, Bluebird, Bloodhound, Blue Fin Tuna, Bluegill, Blue Jay, Blue Whale, Boa, Boar, Bobcat, Boll Weevil, Bonito, Border Collie, Boston Terrier, Boxer, Box Turtle, Brittany Spaniel, Bronco, Brook Trout, Buck, Buffalo, Bug, Bull, Bulldog, Bullfrog, Bull Moose, Bumblebee, Bunny, Burro, Bushmaster, Butterfly, Buzzard

Babushka, Baby Buggy, Backhoe, Backpack, Badminton, Bagpipe, Ballet, Ballet Slippers, Balloon, Ballroom, Band, Bandana, Band Saw, Bandwagon, Banjo, Bank, Bankcard, Bar, Barbecue Pit, Barbed Wire, Barbells, Barn Dance, Barrel, Bar Stool, Barbershop, Bartender, Bat, Basketball, Bassinette, Bassoon, Bat, Bathing Suit, Bathtub Gin, Baton, Battering Ram, Battery, Battle Ax, Battleship, Bayonet, Bazaar, Bazooka, BB Gun, Beach Ball, Bedpan, Beanbag, Beanie, Beaujolais, Beauty Parlor, Bedpan, Beer, Beer Mug, Belfry, Bellbottoms, Bellyache, Belly Dance, Belt Sander, Bentley, Beret, Beriberi, Bib, Bicycle, Bidet, Bifocals, Bikini, Billiards, Billy Club, Bingo, Binoculars, Bistro, Blackberry, Blackjack, Blast Furnace, Blimp, Blindfold, Blizzard, Blockbuster, Blog, Bloody Mary, Bloomers, Blotter, Blouse, Blowgun, Blowtorch, Blunderbuss, BMW, Boat, Bobby

Pin, Bobby Sox, Bobsled, Bodyguard, Bolo, Bomb, Bombshell, Boob Tube, Booby Trap, Bookie, Boom Box, Boomerang, Bootee, Boots, Booze, Borscht, Boutique, Botox, Boudoir, Bourbon, Boutonniere, Bowie Knife, Bowling Ball, Bowtie, Boxcar, Boxing Gloves, Box Kite, Bra, Braille, Break Dance, Brakes, Branding Iron, Brandy, Brass Knuckles, Breathalyzer, Breechcloth, Brew, Briefcase, Brig, Bronchitis, Broom, Bubblegum, Buckshot, Budget, Buggy, Buggy Whip, Bugle, Buick, Bulldozer, Bullet, Bullhorn, Bullet Train, Bull Fiddle, Bull Whip, Bungalow, Bungee Jump, Bunk Bed, Bureaucrat, Burlesque, Bunny Slippers, Bursitis, Bus, Business Card, Bustle, Butcher, Butcher Knife, Buzz Saw, BVD

Calf, Calamari, Calico Cat, Canadian Goose, Camel, Canary, Capuchin Monkey, Caribou, Carp, Carrier Pigeon, Cat, Caterpillar, Catfish, King Chares Spaniel, Centipede, Chameleon, Chamois, Cheshire Cat, Cheetah, Chick, Chicken, Chihuahua, Chimpanzee, Chinchilla, Chipmunk, Clam, Clydesdale, Cobra, Cockatiel, Cockatoo, Cocker Spaniel, Cockroach, Cod, Collie, Colt, Condor, Coon, Copperhead, Coral Snake, Cottonmouth, Cottontail, Cougar, Cow, Cowbird, Cowpony, Coyote, Crab, Crane, Crawdad, Crayfish, Cricket, Croaker, Croc, Crocodile, Crow, Cub, Cuckoo Bird, Cutthroat Trout

Cab, Cabaret, Cabernet, Cab Fare, Cable, Cable Car, Caboose, Caddie, Cadillac, Caffeine, Cage, Calaboose, Calamity, Calculator, Calculus, Caldron, Calendar, Calisthenics, Calliope, Calvary, Calypso, Camcorder, Camera, Cancer, Candlestick, Cane, Cannon, Canoe, Cannonball, Canteen, Cap, Cape, Cappuccino, Carafe, Caravan, Carbine, Carousel, Carburetor, Career, Carpenter, Carpool, Carnival, Car Pool, Cartridge, Cash, Casino, Casket, Castanets, Castle, Catacomb, Catamaran, Catapult, Cataract, Cathedral, Catnip, Cattle Prod, Cauldron, Caviar, CD, Cello, Cell Phone, Cemetery, Chablis, Chain, Chain Gang, Chainsaw, Chairlift, Champagne, Chalet, Chamber Pot, Chandelier, Chaperone, Chapeau, Chardonnay, Chariot, Charley Horse, Chastity Belt, Chauffeur, Chaw, Checkbook, Checkers, Cheerleader, Cheroot, Chess, Chevrolet, Chianti, Chisel, Chrysler, Chiropractor, Chloroform, Chop Sticks, Cigar, Cigarette, Cirrhosis, Cistern, Citizenship, Clarinet, Claw Hammer, Clay Pigeon, Cleaver, Clock, Clodhoppers, Clone, Clorox, Closet, Clown, Club, Cluster Bomb, Coat Rack, Cockpit, Cocktail, Cocktail Party, Coffee

Break, Coffee Mug, Coffin, Cognac, Collateral, College, Coloring Book, Cologne, Coma, Comb, Combat, Comic Book, Commode, Compass, Computer, Confetti, Concert, Congress, Constipation, Consultant, Contract, Convertible, Cookbook, Cooley Hat, Corncob Pipe, Corkscrew, Cornet, Coronary, Coroner, Corsage, Corset, Corvette, Cosmetics, Cosmologist, Cosmonaut, Cotton Gin, Costume, Country Club, Cowboy Boots, Cowboy Hat, Cowbell, CPA, Crabgrass, Cradle, Crank, Crash Helmet, Crash Pad, Crayon, Creampuff, Credit Card, Crematory, Crew Cut, Crib, Cricket, Crime, Critic, Croquet, Crossbow, Crowbar, Crown, Cruise Control, Cruise Missile, Crutches, Crypt, Crying Towel, Cuckoo Clock, Cufflink, Cummerbund, Curb Appeal, Curfew, Cuspidor, Cutlass, Cyanide, Cyclone, Cyclotron, Cymbal, Czar

Dachshund, Daddy Longlegs, Dalmatian, Damselfish, Damselfly, Deer, Deerfly, Deerhound, Deer Mouse, Devilfish, Diamondback, Dik dik, Dingo, Dinosaur, Doberman, Doe, Dog, Dolphin, Donkey, Dormouse, Dove, Dover Sole, Draft Horse, Dragonfly, Drake, Duck, Duck-billed Platypus, Duckling, Dungeness Crab

Dagger, Daiquiri, Dandruff, Dart, Daycare, DDT, Deadbolt, Debt, Debut, Decorator, Decoy, Defoliant, Defroster, Degree, Dental Floss, Dentist, Dentures, Depth Charge, Derringer, Designer Diapers, Desk, Detonator, Detoxification, Deutschemark, Dexedrine, Diabetes, Diamond, Diaper, Diarrhea, Diary, Dice, Dictionary, Diesel, Dinghy, Dinner Bell, Diploma, Dip Net, Dipstick, Diphtheria, Dirigible, Dirt Bike, Disciple, Disco, Discus, Disease, Disguise, Dishtowel, Distillery, Diving Board, Divorce, Dobro, Dock, Doily, Doll House, Dominos, Doorbell, Doorknob, Doormat, Dormitory, Dragnet, Dragster, Drano, Drapes, Drawers, Dreadlock, Dress, Dress Code, Drill, Drone, Drought, Drugstore, Drum, Duct Tape, Duel, Duffle Bag, Dulcimer, Dumpster, Dump Truck, Dunce Cap, Dungarees, Dungeon, Dust Bunny, Dynamite

Eagle, Eaglet, Earthworm, Eel, Egret, Eland, Electric Eel, Elephant, Elephant Seal, Elk, Elkhound, Emperor Penguin, Emu, Ermine, English Setter, Eskimo Dog, Ewe

Earache, Earmuffs, Earplug, Earrings, Earthquake, Easel, Éclair, Eggbeater, Electric Chair, Electric Eye, Elevator, Editor, Email, Emergency Brake, Emery Board, Encyclopedia, Enema, Enemy, English, Emphysema, Encyclopedia, Entourage, Epee, Epitaph, Eraser, Erector Set, Escalator, Escort, Etiquette, Euros, Evening Gown, Executioner, Executive, Exile, Ex-lax, Expense Account, Explosion, Exterminator, Eye Shadow

Falcon, Fawn, Fer-de-lance, Feral Hog, Ferret, Fiddler Crab, Field Mouse, Filly, Finch, Fire Ant, Firefly, Fish, Fish Hawk, Flamingo, Flea, Flounder, Fly Flying Fish, Flying Squirrel, Foal, Fox, Fox Hound, Fox Terrier, Frog, Fruit Fly

Facebook, Facelift, Face Paint, Facial, Factory, Fair, Faith, False Teeth, Fanny Pack, Fax, FBI, Featherbed, Feather Boa, Feather Duster, Fedora, Fed X, Fender, Ferrari, Ferris Wheel, Ferryboat, Fertilizer, Festival, Fever, Fez, Fiction, Fiddle, Fiddlestick, Fiesta, Fife, Fight, Figure Skates, Filibuster, Filleting Knife, Finance, Finger Paint, Fire Alarm, Firearm, Firecracker, Fire Drill, Fire Escape, Fire Extinguisher, Fire Hose, Fire Hydrant, Fireplace, Fire Truck, Fireworks, Firing Pin, Firing Squad, Fishing License, Fishing Pole, Flag, Flak Jacket, Flame Thrower, Flare, Flashbulb, Flashlight, Flask, Flight Plan Flintlock, Flood, Floodlight, Flophouse, Florist, Floss, Flowerpot, Flu, Flugelhorn, Flute, Flypaper, Fly Rod, Flyswatter, Foghorn, Food Stamps, Fog Horn, Football, Footie Pajamas, Footlocker, Footstool, Foreclosure, Fork, Forklift, Formaldehyde, Forrest Fire, Fort, Fortress, Fortune, Fountain Pen, Foxhole, Freezer, Freight Car, Freight Train, Freighter, French, French Horn, Freon, Frisbee, Frock, Frostbite, Frying Pan, Fuel Cell, Funeral, Funnel, Furnace, Furrier, Fuse, Futon, Fairway

Gamecock, Gander, Gar, Garter Snake, Gar, Gator, Gazelle, Gecko, Gerbil, German Shepherd, Giant Panda, Giant Squid, Gila Monster, Giraffe, Glassfish, Glowworm, Gnat, Gnu, Goat, Golden Eagle, Golden Retriever, Golden Trout, Goldfinch, Goldfish,

Gaffe, Gag, Gallows, Gallstone, Galoshes, Gangrene, Gangplank, Gaff, Garage Sale, Garret, Garter, Garter Belt, Gas Mask, Gasoline, Gatling Gun, Gavel, Gazebo, Geiger Counter, Gem, Gemstone, Geyser, GI, Gig, Gimlet, Gin, Gin Rummy, Girdle, Glacie

Goose, Gopher, Gorilla, Gosling, Grackle, Grasshopper, Gray Wolf, Great Dane, Great White Shark, Green Snake, Green Turtle, Grey Fox, Greyhound, Grizzly Bear, Groundhog, Grouper, Grouse, Guide Dog, Guinea Hen, Guinea Pig, Guppy, Gull, Gypsy Moth

r, Glider, Global Warming, Glockenspiel, Glue, Glove, Glue, Goalpost, Goatee, Go Cart, Goggles, Gold, Golf, Golf Cart, Golf Clubs, Golf Course, Gondola, Google, Gourmet, Gout, GPS, Grandstand, Grammar, Graveyard, Grenade, Greasy Spoon, Griddle, Grill, Grog, Guillotine, Guitar, Gun, Gunboat, Gunnysack, Gutter, Gutter Ball, Gym, Gymnasium, Gym Shoes, Gyroscope

Haddock, Halibut, Hammerhead, Hamster, Hard Shell Clam, Hare, Harp Seal, Hartebeest, Hatchet Fish, Hawk, Hedgehog, Heifer, Hen, Hermit Crab, Herring, Heron, Hippo, Hog, Hognose Snake, Holstein, Homing Pigeon, Honey Badger, Honeybee, Hoot Owl, Horned Toad, Hornet, Horse, Horsefly, Horseshoe Crab, Hound, Howler Monkey, Hummingbird, Humpback Whale, Husky, Hyena

Haberdasher, Hacienda, Hacksaw, Hailstorm, Haircut, Hairnet, Hairspray, Hairpiece, Hairpin, Halitosis, Halloween, Halo, Halter, Hammer, Hammock, Handbag, Handcuffs, Hand Grenade, Hand Gun, Hanky, Handkerchief, Hanger, Hang Glider, Hangnail, Hangover, Halloween, Happy Hour, Hard Hat, Hardware, Harley-Davidson, Harmonica, Harness, Harp, Harpoon, Harpsichord, Hat, Hat Rack, Hatchback, Hatchet, Headlight, Hearing Aid, Hearse, Heart Attack, Heatstroke, Helicopter, Helmet, Hemlock, Hemophilia, Hen House, Herbicide, Hernia, Hibachi, Hiccups, Hi-Fi, Highball, Highchair, High Heels, Hip Boots, Hipflask, Hobby, Hobbyhorse, Hockey Stick, Hockey Puck, Hoe, Hollow Point, Hollywood, Holster, Honda, Honeymoon, Honey Wagon, Honky-tonk, Hooch, Hook Shot, Hoosegow, Hootenanny, Horn, Horoscope, Horseradish, Horsewhip, Hot Toddy, Hot Rod, Hot Tub, Hourglass, Houseboat, Hovel, Hovercraft, Howitzer, Hubcap, Hula Hoop, Humidor, Hummer, Hunter, Hunting Knife, Hunting License, Hurricane, Hydroplane

Ibex, Ibis, Iguana, Impala, Inchworm, Insect, Irish Setter

I-Beam, Ice, Iceberg, Icebox, Ice Pick, Icicle, Ice Skates, Idol, Igloo, Incarceration, Incense, Incinerator, Incubator, Incinerator, Infantry, Inferiority Complex, Inferno, Inflation, Influenza, Inheritance, Ink, Inkjet, Inn, Inner Tube, Insecticide, Insomnia, Insurance, Internet, IOU, i-phone, iPod, Iron, Ironing board, Italian, Ivory tower

Jackal, Jackass, Jackrabbit, Jaguar, Jay, Javelina, Jellyfish, June Bug

Jacuzzi, Jack, Jacket, Jackhammer, Jack-in-the-box, Jackknife, Jack-o-lantern, Jackpot, Jai-alai, Jail, Jalopy, Jamboree, Japanese, Jaundice, Javelin, Jawbreaker, Jazz, Jeep, Jellybean, Jet, Jetlag, Jet Ski, Jewelry, Jewels, Jigsaw, Job, Jockey, Jock Itch, Jodhpurs, Jockstrap, Joyride, Jubilee, Judo, Ju-jitsu, Jukebox, Jumper Cables, Jump Rope, Jumpsuit, Jungle Gym, Junk Bond, Junk Mail, Jury, Jupiter

Kangaroo, Kangaroo Rat, Killer Bee, Killer Whale, Komodo Dragon, King Cobra, King Crab, Kingfish, Kingfisher, King Salmon, King Bird, King Snake, King Vulture, Kit Fox, Kitten, Kiwi, Koala, Kodiak Koi, Krill

Kahlua, Kaleidoscope, Karate, Kayak, Kazoo, Keel, Keg, Kerosene, Ketch, Kettle, Kettledrum, Key, Keyboard, Kickball, Kidney Stone, Kiln, Kilt, Kimono, Kindergarten, Kiosk, Kite, Kleenex, Kleptomania, K-Mart, Knapsack, Kneepads, Knee Socks, Knickers, Knife, Kodak, Kung fu

Labrador Retriever, Ladybug, Lake Trout, Lamb, Lamprey, Lapdog, Largemouth Bass, Lark, Leech, Leghorn, Lemming, Lemon Shark, Lemon Sole, Lemur, Leopard, Leopard Seal, Lhasa Apso, Lice, Lightning Bug, Ling, Lion, Lion Fish, Lipizzaner, Lizard, Llama, Lobster, Locust, Loggerhead Turtle, Longhorn, Loon, Louse, Love Bird, Lynx

Label, Laboratory, Lace, La cross, Ladder, Ladle, Lamp, Lampshade, Lance, Landfill, Landing Gear, Land Mine, Land Rover, Landslide, Lantern, Lariat, Laryngitis, Laser, Lasso, Latrine, Laughing Gas, Laugh Track, Laundromat, Lavatory, Law Degree, Lawnmower, Laxative, Leash, Leavenworth, Leggings, Lectern, Legerdemain, Lei, Lemonade, Leotards, Leukemia, Levis, Lexus, Librarian, Library, Lie Detector, Lifeboat, Life Insurance, Lifejacket, Life Raft, Lighthouse, Lightning Rod, Limousine, Lingerie, Liposuction, Lipstick, Liquor, Liquor Store, Literature, Lumberjack, Lock, Lockjaw, Locomotive, Logo, Loincloth, Lollypop, Longbow, Long Johns, Loom, Looney Bin, Lottery, Lotto, Luau, Luggage, Luger, Lute, Lyre, Lyricist

Macaw, Mackerel, Maggot, Magpie, Mako Shark, Malamute, Mallard, Mamba, Manatee, Man-o-war, Manta Ray, Manx Cat, Mare, Marlin, Marmoset, Martin, Maverick, Mayfly, Meadowlark, Meer Kat, Milk Snake, Millipede, Mink, Minnow, Mockingbird,

Maalox, Mace, Machete, Machinegun, Magnet, Magnifying Glass, Mai Tai, Makeup, Malaria, Mall, Mallet, Manacles, Mandolin, Manhattan, Manicure, Mannequin, Mansion, Manuscript, Map, Marathon, Margarita, Marimba, Marina, Marine,

Mole, Monarch Butterfly, Mongoose, Mongrel, Monkey, Moose, Moray Eel, Mosquito, Mosquito Hawk, Moth, Mountain Goat, Mountain Lion, Mourning Dove, Mouse, Mudpuppy, Mule, Mule Deer, Mullet, Musk Ox, Muskrat, Musky, Mussel, Mustang, Myna Bird

Marksman, Martini, Mascara, Mascot, Mask, Masking Tape, Mast, Matador, Matches, Matrimony, Mattress, Mazda, Maze, Measles, Medical School, Medicare, Megaphone, Memoir, MENSA, Mentor, Menu, Mercedes, Merry-go-round, Meteor, Mickey Finn, Microphone, Microscope, Microwave, Migraine, Militia, Minefield, Miniskirt, Mint Julep, Minuet, Mirror, Missile, Mistletoe, Mittens, Mixmaster, Model A, Mohawk, Molotov Cocktail, Money Belt, Monocle, Monorail, Monsoon, Moonshine, Mop, Moped, Morgue, Morphine, Motel, Mortgage, Morgue, Mortar, Mortician, Motorcycle, Mountain Bike, Mousetrap, Moustache, Mouthwash, Mud Flaps, Muffler, Musket, Mustache, Muzak, Muzzle

Nanny Goat, Needlefish, Nene, Neon Tetra, Newt, Night Crawler, Night Hawk, Nightingale, Northern Pike, Nutria

Nail, Nail File, Nail Polish, Napalm, Napkin, NASCAR, Navigator, Navy, Necklace, Necktie, Needle, Negligee, Newspaper, Nerf Ball, Net, Nickelodeon, Nicotine, Nightclub, Nightgown, Nightmare, Nine Iron, Nitroglycerin, Nobel Prize, Noose, Notary, Notebook, Novel, NRA, Nuke, Nursemaid

Ocelot, Octopus, Old English Sheepdog, Opossum, Orangutan, Orca, Oriole, Osprey, Ostrich, Otter, Owl, Owlet, Ox, Oyster

Oar, Oasis, Obi, Obituary, Oboe, Odometer, Office, Oil Well, Old-fashioned, Oldsmobile, Old Spice, Opal, Opera, Opera Glasses, Orchestra, Organ, Organ Grinder, Ottoman, Ouija board, Outhouse, Oven, Overalls, Overcoat, Overshoes

Packrat, Palomino, Panda, Panther, Parakeet, Parrot, Partridge, Passenger Pigeon, Peacock, Peahen, Peccary, Pekinese, Pelican, Penguin, Perch, Peregrine, Persian Cat, Pheasant, Pickerel, Pig, Pigeon, Piglet, Pike, Pileated Woodpecker, Pilot Fish, Pilot Whale, Pinto, Piranha, Pit Bull, Polar Bear, Polecat, Polliwog, Polo Pony, Pomeranian, Pompano, Pony, Poodle, Porcupine, Porpoise, Possum, Potbellied Pig, Prairie Chicken, Prairie Dog, Prawn, Praying

Pacemaker, Pacifier, Paddle, Paddy Wagon, Padlock, Pajamas, Pager, Paint, Paintbrush, Panties, Pajamas, Palace, Pallbearer, Pantaloons, Pantyhose, Paperclip, Parachute, Parade, Paralysis, Paranoia, Parasite, Parasol, Parole, Parka, Party Hat, Passport, Pawnshop, Payroll, Pearl, Peashooter, Pedestal, Pedicure, Pedigree, Pedometer, Peep Show, Peg Leg, Pencil, Penitentiary, Pinochle, Penthouse, Pepper, Peppermill, Pepper Spray, Percolator, Perdition, Perfume, Periscope, Peroxide,

Mantas, Pronghorn, Puff Adder, Puffer Fish, Puffin, Pug, Pullet, Puma, Puppy, Purple Finch, Pygmy Goat, Pygmy Owl, Pygmy Whale, Python

Periscope, Pesos, Pesticide, Petunia, Petticoat, Ph.D. Philosophy, Phone, Physics, Phrenology, Piano, Picador, Piccolo, Pickax, Pickpocket, Pickup Truck, Pile Driver, Pilot, Pinafore, Piñata, Pinball Machine, Pincushion, Ping Pong, Pink Sheet, Pinochle, Pinot Greggio, Pitch Pipe, Pistol, Pit Boss, Pitchfork, Pitch Pipe, Placebo, Plague, Plane, Platinum, *Playboy*, Plow, Plumber, Pneumonia, Pocketknife, Podium, Poetry, Pogo Stick, Poison Ivy, Poker, Polo, Pole Vault, Pollution, Portfolio, Politics, Polygraph, Pompom, Poncho, Pontiac, Pontoon, Pool Table, Popgun, Port, Portrait, Post Nasal Drip, Potty Seat, Pouilly Fuissee, Powder Keg, Powdered Wig, Power Plant, Powder Puff, Predator, President, Press Agent, Press Box, Prison, Privy, Proctologist, Profession, Professor, Propeller, Punching Bag, Psychiatrist, Pub, Pulpit, Punchbowl, Punching Bag, Puppet, Purgatory, Pup Tent, Purse, Putter, Putting Green, Puzzle, Pyramid

Quahog, Quail, Quarter Horse, Quetzal

Q-tip, Quack, Quagmire, Quarrel, Quarterback, Quicksand, Quill, Quilt, Quiver, Quonset Hut

Rabbit, Raccoon, Racehorse, Rainbow Trout, Ram, Raptor, Rat, Rat Snake, Rattlesnake, Raven, Razorback, Red Ant, Red Billed Woodpecker, Redbird, Red Breasted Woodpecker, Redfish, Red Fox, Redheaded Woodpecker, Red Snapper, Red Wolf, Reebok, Reef Shark, Reindeer, Rhesus Monkey, Rhino, Ribbonfish, Ridley Turtle, River Otter, Roadrunner, Robin, Rock Bass, Rockfish, Rock Lobster, Rodent, Rooster, Rottweiler

Rabies, Racetrack, Radar, Radio, Raffle, Raft, Railroad, Raincoat, Rake, Rapier, Rap Sheet, Rash, Rasp, Rathskeller, Rattle, Razor, Reel, Referee, Reformatory, Refrigerator, Regatta, Rehab, Rheostat, Region, Rehab, Rembrandt, Renminbi, Resort, Resume, Revolution, Revolver, Riata, Rickshaw, Rifle, Rigor Mortis, Riot, Ripcord, Ripsaw, Ritalin, Road Grater, Roadster, Robot, Rocker, Rocket, Rocking Chair, Rodeo, Roller Coaster, Roller Skates, Rolling Pin, Rolls Royce, Rolodex, Root Canal, ROTC, Rotisserie, Rototiller, Rouge, Roulette, Royalty, Rowboat, Rubbles, Ruby, Rudder, Rugby, Rum, Rupee, Russian Roulette

Saber Tooth Tiger, Sable, Sailfish, Saint Bernard, Salamander, Salmon, Sand Dollar, Sand Fly, Sand Hill Crane, Sandpiper, Sardine, Savanna Cat, Sawfish, Scallop, Schnauzer, Schnook, Scorpion, Scotty, Screech Owl, Scrod, Sea Anemone, Sea Bass, Sea Cow, Sea Eagle, Seagull, Seahawk, Seahorse, Seal, Sea Lion, Sea Otter, Sea Slug, Sea Snake, Sea Trout, Sea Urchin, Seeing-eye Dog, Shad, Shark, Sheep, Sheepdog, Shellfish, Sheltie, Shetland Pony, Shetland Sheepdog, Shrew, Shrimp, Siamese Cat, Siberian Tiger, Sidewinder, Silkworm, Silverback, Silver Fox, Simian, Skunk, Skylark, Sled Dog, Sloth, Slug, Smelt, Snail, Snail Darter, Snake, Snapping Turtle, Snipe, Snow Goose, Snow Leopard, Snowshoe Hare, Snowy Owl, Sockeye, Sow, Sparrow, Speckled Trout, Sperm Whale, Spider, Spider Monkey, Springbok, Springer Spaniel, Spoonbill Cat, Spring Chicken, Sphynx Cat, Squid, Squirrel, Stag, Stallion, Starfish, Starling, Steelhead, Steenbok, Steer, Stink Bug, Stingray, Stork, Sturgeon, Sunfish, Swallow, Swan, Swine, Swordfish

Sabbatical, Saber Saw, Saber, Sack, Saddle, Saddlebag, Saddle Soap, Safari, Safe, Safety Belt, Safety Pin, Safety Shoes, Sail, Sailboat, Sake, Salon, Saloon, Sampan, Sandals, Sandblaster, Sandpaper, Sapphire, Saran Wrap, Sari, Sarong, Sarsaparilla, Sash, Satellite Dish, Saturn, Saucer, Sauna, Saw, Sawhorse, Saxophone, Scaffold, Scale, Scalpel, Scapegoat, Scarecrow, School Bus, Scissors, Scooter, Scotch, Scotch Tape, Scow, Scurvy, Scaffold, Scrapbook, Screwdriver, Scythe, Searchlight, Seatbelt, Secretary, Seesaw, Senility, Senate, Septic Tank, Settee, Sewing Machine, Sex Education, Shackles, Shampoo, Shanty, Shave, Shaving Cream, Shawl, Shield, Shillelagh, Shish Kabob, Shock Absorber, Shoe Laces, Shoe Polish, Shot Glass, Shot Put, Shotgun, Shoulder Pads, Shovel, Shrapnel, Shrink, Shuffleboard, Shuttlecock, Sickle, Sidearm, Silicone, Silk Socks, Silly Putty, Silo, Silver, Silverware, Singapore Sling, Sing-Sing, Siren, Sitar, Six-pack, Skateboard, Skeet, Skeleton Key, Skewer, Ski, Skid Row, Ski Lift, Skillet, Skirt, Skivvies, Sky Blue Pink Bloomers, Skybox, Skylight, Skyscraper, Slaughterhouse, Sledgehammer, Sleeping Bag, Sleeping Pills, Sleet, Sleigh, Sleigh Bed, Slingshot, Slip, Slippers, Sloppy Joe, Slot Machine, Smallpox, Smog, Smokehouse, Smokestack, Snail Mail, Snare, Snare Drum, Sneakers, Snorkel, Snow Shovel, Snow Plow, Snowshoes, Snowball, Snowmobile, Soapbox, Soccer, Socks, Softball, Software, Solitaire Sombrero, Sonar, Spa, Spaceship, Spade, Spam, Spanish, Spare Tire, Sparkplug, Spats, Spatula, Spear, Speedboat, Speedo, Speedometer, Spike Heels, Spikes, Spinning Wheel, Spitball, Spittoon, Spotlight, Spot Remover, Spray Paint, Spur, Squad Car, Squawk Box, Squall, Squeegee, Squirt Gun,

Stable, Stadium, Stage, Stagecoach, Stamp, Stampede, Starbucks, Stationery, Statue, Steam Iron, Steam Shovel, Steamboat, Steamroller, Steel Wool, Stein, Stepladder, Sterling, Sterno, Stethoscope, Stetson, Stiletto, Still, Stilts, Stirrup, Stockade, Stockcar, Stock Market, Stogie, Stomachache, Stopwatch, Straightjacket, Strip Chess, Stretch Pants, Striptease, Subway, Sunlamp, Stilts, Strongbox, Stove, Stradivari, Straightjacket, Strep Throat, Stretch Pants, Stretcher, Stiletto, Stiletto Heels, Stirrups, String Tie, Strip Mine, Strip Poker, Stroller, Strychnine, Stun Gun, Submarine, Subway, Suit, Suitcase, Sumo Wrestling, Sundial, Sunglasses, Sunlamp, Sunscreen, Supercollider, Surfboard, Surround Sound, Suspenders, Sweater, Sweat Socks, Sweat suit, Swill, Swimsuit, Swing, Swivel Chair, Swizzle Stick, Sword, Synfuel

Tabby Cat, Tadpole, Tapeworm, Tapir, Tarantula, Tarpon, Tasmanian Devil, Teal, Termite, Terrapin, Tic, Tiger, Tiger Shark, Tiger Shrimp, Tilapia, Timber Wolf, Titmouse, Toad, Tomcat, Tortoise, Toucan, Toy Fox Terrier, Trigger Fish, Tree Frog, Tree Swallow, Tree Toad, Trout, Trumpeter Swan, Tsetse Fly, Tuna, Turkey, Turkey Buzzard, Turkey Vulture, Turtle, Turtle Dove

Tabasco, Table Manners, Tachometer, Tack Hammer, Taillight, Tailor, Tambourine, Tank, Tankard, Tantrum, Tape Deck, Tape Recorder, Tar Pit, Taser, Tassel, Tattoo, Tavern, Taxi, Tax Break, Taxidermist, Teacup, Teapot, Tea Set, Teaspoon, Teargas, Teeter Tauter, Teething Ring, Telephone, Teleprompter, Telescope, Telethon, Television, Tendinitis, Tennis, Tennis Racquet, Tepee, Tequila, Tether, Theater, Thermostat, Thesaurus, Thimble, Thong, Throne, Throttle, Thumbscrew, Thumbtack, Thunderbird, Thunder Mug, Tiara, Tickertape, Tiddlywinks, Tie Rack, Tights, Tightrope, Time Bomb, Time Clock, Tinker Toy, Tin Lizzy, Tires, Tire Iron, TNT, Tobacco, Toboggan, Toe-tag, Toga, Toilet Paper, Tomahawk, Tomb, Tombstone, Tommy Gun, Tom-tom, Toothache, Toothpaste, Tool Chest, Tool Kit, Toothpick, Top Hat, Torch, Toreador, Tornado, Torpedo, Totem Pole, Toupee, Tow Truck, Track Shoes, Tractor, Trailer, Train, Trail Bike, Trampoline, Tranquilizer, Trap, Trapper, Trapdoor,

Trapeze, Trawler, Treadmill, Trench Coat, Tricycle, Trigger, Trigonometry, Trolley, Trotline, Trombone, Trousers, Trousseau, Trowel, Truck, Trumpet, Trunk, Truth Serum, TSA, Tsunami, Tuba, Tugboat, Tummy Tuck, Tune Up, Turbine, Turn Kit, Tutor, Turban, Turnpike, Turnstile, Turntable, Turtleneck, Turpentine, Tutu, Tuxedo, Tweezers, Twinkies, Twitter, Typewriter, Typhoon

nil

U-boat, Ukulele, Ulcer, Umbrella, Umpire, Underpants, Underskirt, Undertaker, Underwear, Unicycle, Uniform, Union, University, UPS, Uranium, Urinal, Urn, User ID, U-tube, Uzi

Vampire Bat, Vampire Squid, Varmint, Vicuña, Viper, Vole, Vulture

Vacuum Cleaner, Valentine, Valet, Valise, Valium, Van, Vanity Case, Vasectomy, Vault, Vaudeville, VCR, Vehicle, Veil, Velcro, Venetian Blinds, Ventriloquist, Vermouth, Vest, Viagra, Vibraphone, Vibrator, Vice, Vichyssoise, Videotape, Vinegar, Virus, Voice Mail, Viola, Violin, Virus, Visa, Vise, Vivisectionist, Vocation, Vodka, Voicemail, Volcano, Volleyball, Volt, Volvo, Voodoo, Vote

Wallaby, Walleye, Walrus, Wapiti, Warthog, Wasp, Watchdog, Water Beetle, Water Buck, Water Buffalo, Water Moccasin, Weasel, Weevel, Whale, Whippet, Whip-poor-will, White Bass, Whitefish, White Tailed Deer, White Whale, Whiting, Whooping Crane, Wild Boar, Wildcat, Wildebeest, Wolf, Wolfhound, Wolf Pack, Wolverine, Wombat, Woodchuck, Woodcock, Wood Duck, Woodpecker, Wood Pussy, Worm, Wren

Waffle Iron, Wagon, Walker, Walkie-talkie, Walking Stick, Wallet, Wallpaper, Wall Street Journal, Street, Wampum, War, War Bonnet, Wardrobe, Wart, Wastebasket, Watch, Waterbed, Water-board, Water Polo, Water Skis, Water Wings, Weapon, Weather Vane, Web Browser, Website, Wedding Cake, Wedding Ring, Weightwatchers, Welfare, Wet Suit, Wheel, Wheelbarrow, Wheelchair, Whip, Whiplash, Whippet, Whirlpool, Whirlwind, Whirlybird, Whiskbroom, Whisky, Whistle, Whoopee Cushion, Wifi, Wig, Wigwam, Will, Winchester, Windmill, Wind Tunnel, Wine Cellar, Wishing Well, Wok, Wooden Leg, Woodshed, Woodwind, Wrecker, Wrecking Bar, Wrench, Wrestling, Wristwatch

Xerox, X-ray, Xylophone

Yak, Yellow Bellied Sap Sucker, Yellow Finch, Yellow Jacket, Yellow Lab, Yorkshire Terrier

Zebra, Zebra Fish, Zebra Mule

Yacht, Yacht Club, Yahoo, Yardstick, Yawl, Yearbook, Yellow Fever, YMCA, Yoga, Yoke, Yoyo, Yuan

Zapper, Zeppelin, Zinfandel, Zip Code, Zip Gun, Zip Loc, Zipper, Zippo, Zircon, Zither, Zoo, Zombie, Zoot Suit, Zydeco

APPENDIX B
RHYME OPTIONS

As previously mentioned, rhyming often contributes to creating clever quips. You can find rhyming candidates in hard copy rhyming dictionaries (Miriam Webster's, for example at $6.50) or free on the net (Rhyme Zone, for example). The problem with both is that wading through them to find words that rhyme with pegs can be time consuming. The purpose of this Appendix is to simplify your searches by listing pivots that rhyme with each of the pegs in Appendix A. Following is an example of how it's constructed.

Butterfly alibi, apple pie, barfly, battle cry, black eye, bolo tie, bowtie, buckeye, **butterfly**, cow pie, deadeye, **dragonfly**, electric eye, FBI, **firefly**, gadfly, GI, hawk eye, hi-fi, jai-alai, lullaby, **magpie**, mai tai, necktie, pigsty, pinkeye, private eye, railroad tie, RBI, semi, string tie, tie dye, **tsetse fly**, **walleye**, wise guy

When animals are shown in bold like dragonfly, firefly, magpie, tsetse fly and walleye above, it indicates that there are separate listings for them.

Aardvark	amusement park, ballpark, Cutty Sark, Deutschemark, ear mark, **lark,** Makers Mark, **meadowlark, monarch**, narc, national park, **shark, skylark**, theme park, **tiger shark**
Abalone	alimony, macaroni, matrimony, palimony, pepperoni, **pony**, spumoni
Afghan Hound	**basset hound, bloodhound, dachshund, deer hound, elk hound,** dog pound, end around, fair ground, **fox hound**, greyhound, lost and found, merry-go-round, surround-sound, **wolfhound**
Airedale	brail, **Clydesdale,** coattail, cocktail, cocktail, **cottontail**, e-mail, fairytale, ginger ale, hangnail, jail, junk mail, **killer whale**, monorail, nail mail, nail, **nightingale**, pigtail, **pilot whale**, ponytail, **pygmy whale, quail**, sail, scale, **snail**, snail mail, **sperm whale**, tattletale, vapor trail, veil, voicemail, **whale**
Akita	**Cheetah,** fajita, margarita, senorita

Albacore
ambassador, bed sore, **boar**, book store, commodore, **condor**, cuspidor, drug store, fire door, humidor, **Labrador**, liquor store, **man-o-war**, matador, mentor, memoir, oar, parquet floor, picador, pinafore, **raptor,** Realtor, revolving door, saddle sore, storm door, swinging door, toreador, troubadour, war

Albatross
boss, dental floss, lacrosse, moss, motor cross, pit boss, straw boss

Alley Cat
autocrat, **bobcat**, bureaucrat, **calico cat**, coolie hat, copycat, cowboy hat, dingbat, diplomat, doormat, fungo bat, hard hat, laundromat, **mare, meer kat**, mud flap, **muskrat**, place mat, **polecat**, porkpie hat, **rat**, rheostat, **s**iamese cat, silk hat, **tabby cat**, technocrat, **Savannah cat, tomcat**, top hat, **vampire bat**, welcome mat, **wildcat, wombat**

Alligator
accelerator, arbitrator, aviator, calculator, carburetor, crater, decorator, detonator, dumb waiter, escalator, elevator, exterminator, radiator, prevaricator, refrigerator, tailgater, vibrator

Alligator Gar
armoire, armored car, bazaar, boudoir, boxcar, bumper car, candy bar, cattle car, cigar, crowbar, czar, film star, freight car, **gar**, guitar, **jaguar**, muscle car, pace car, radar, side car, sitar, scar, sleeping car, sonar, sports car, squad car, steel guitar, tank car, T-bar, tool bar, muscle car, pace car, pine tar, sleeping car, sonar steel guitar, streetcar, squad car, VCR, wine bar, wrecking bar

Alligator Lizard
blizzard, gizzard, wizard

Alpaca
nil

Amoeba
nil

Anaconda
Honda, Uganda, veranda

Anchovy
nil

Angelfish
baking dish, **angelfish**, billfish, **catfish, codfish, crawfish**, damselfish, death wish, fetish, finfish, **goldfish, jellyfish, kingfish**, lionfish, Petri dish, **redfish, rockfish, sailfish**, satellite dish, **sawfish, shellfish**, soap dish, **swordfish, triggerfish, whitefish**, Yiddish

Angleworm	accounting firm, germ, law firm, pachyderm, perm, prison term, **pachyderm**,
Angora Cat	see **Alley Cat**
Angora Goat	banknote, C-note, **coyote**, creosote, dreamboat, ferryboat, gunboat, houseboat, iceboat, lab coat, lifeboat, **mountain goat**, **nanny goat**, pea coat, petticoat, rowboat, sailboat, speedboat, steamboat, strep throat, T-note, torpedo boat, trench coat, tugboat, U-boat, vote
Ant	assailant, confidant, consultant, defoliant, deodorant, **elephant**, **fire ant**, fire hydrant, giant, implant, intoxicant, pendant, power plant, spider plant, stretch pant, transplant, underpants
Anteater	Beefeater, egg beater, heater, two-seater.
Antelope	bunny slope, gyroscope, horoscope, jump rope, kaleidoscope, microscope, periscope, stethoscope, telescope, tight rope
Ape	adhesive tape, audiotape, cape, drape, duct tape, fire escape, masking tape, red tape, Scotch tape, tickertape, videotape
Appaloosa	Tuskaloosa
Arabian Horse	air force, charley horse, clotheshorse, divorce, golf course, hobbyhorse, **Horse**, obstacle course, **quarter horse**, racecourse, sawhorse, **seahorse**, task force
Arctic Fox	ballot box, bobby socks, boom box, boondocks, Botox, cuckoo clock, dreadlocks, flintlock, **Fox**, grandfather clocks, idiot box, jack-in-the-box, jukebox, mailbox, **musk ox**, **ox**, Pandora's box, pillbox, press box, safe deposit box, sandbox, shamrocks, shot clocks, shuttlecocks, skybox, smallpox, soapbox, socks, squawk box, stocks, strongbox, toolbox, Xerox
Armadillo	Brillo, cigarillo, peccadillo, pillow, willow
Asp	clasp, handclasp, rasp

Ass **bass,** bluegrass, brass, crabgrass, gas, glass, **jackass,** salt grass, shot glass, spyglass, stained glass, teargas, laughing gas, lemongrass, wineglass

Atlantic Salmon **Tarpon**

Baboon bassoon, balloon, buffoon, cartoon, cocoon, **coon,** goon, greasy spoon, harpoon, honeymoon, lagoon, **loon,** monsoon, pantaloon, platoon, pontoon, **raccoon,** saloon, sand dune, silver spoon, spittoon, trial balloon, tycoon, typhoon

Badger nil

Bald eagle paralegal

Baltimore Oriel nil

Bantam Rooster booster

Barnacle nil

Barn Owl beach towel, crying towel, night owl, **screech owl, snowy owl,** tea towel, trowel, Turkish towel, **waterfowl**

Barracuda Bermuda, Buddha

Bass **Ass**

Basset Hound see Afghan Hound

Bat see **Alley Cat**

Beagle see **Bald Eagle**

Bear air fare, armchair, boutonniere, chair, electric chair, day care, fair, flare, **hare,** highchair, lawn chair, potty-chair, **mare,** Medicare, **polar bear,** rocking chair, silverware, snare, software, swivel chair, underwear, welfare, wheelchair

Beaver cantilever, cleaver, fever, **golden retriever,** reliever, weaver, wide receiver

Bedbug	bear hug, **bedbug**, coffee mug, fireplug, jitterbug, **ladybug**, **lightning bug**, litterbug, oriental rug, prayer rug, **Sea Slug,** spark plug.
Bee	BB, **bumblebee**, artillery, bikini, biscotti, Chablis, chamois, chili, **chimpanzee**, Christmas tree, church key, college degree, daiquiri, DDT, epee, factory, Ferrari, fleur-de-lis, Frisbee, goatee, golf tee, grease monkey, greens fee, hemlock tree, hibachi, **honeybee, husky,** iced tea, jamboree, **killer bee, kiwi**, law degree, lingerie, LSD, machete, maitre d', **manatee**, martini, pass key, pedigree, privy, referee, renmimbi, rotisserie, Saki, shoe tree, skeleton key, snow ski, spaghetti, squeegee, tepee, TNT, trick knee, water ski
Beetle	nil
Beluga Whale	see **Airedale**
Bengal Tiger	**saber toothed tiger, Siberian tiger, tiger**
Bighorn	bullhorn, English horn, flugelhorn, foghorn, French horn, greenhorn, **leghorn, longhorn**, morn, popcorn, powder horn, saddle horn, shoehorn, thorn, uniform
Billy Goat	see **Angora Goat**
Bird	**bluebird,** buzzword, crossword, **hummingbird,** jailbird, **mockingbird,** password, **redbird,** swearword, Thunderbird, whirlybird
Birddog	blog, **bulldog, bullfrog,** catalog, **dog, frog,** grog, **groundhog, hog,** leapfrog, **pollywog, prairie dog, sheepdog,** smog, travelogue, **tree frog, warthog,** Yule log
Bird of Paradise	nil
Blackbird	see **Bird**
Black Drum	**a**trium, asylum, conundrum, drum, kettle drum, rum, tantrum
Black Lab	**Yellow Lab**
Black Mamba	**Mamba**

Black Squirrel	ball girl, bat girl, Campfire girl, chorus girl, cover girl, cowgirl, girl, flower girl, **flying squirrel**, mother-of-pearl, mural, pearl, pin curl, pinup girl, playgirl, **Squirrel**, sweater girl
Black Vulture	agriculture, aquaculture, aviculture, culture, counterculture, **king vulture, turkey vulture,** horticulture, viniculture, **vulture,**
Black Widow Spider	bareback rider, bull rider, glider, hang glider, rodeo rider
Bluebird	see **Bird**
Bloodhound	see **Afghan Hound**
Blue Fin Tuna	nil
Bluegill	chill, fire drill, **gerbil**, grille, **krill,** landfill, molehill, oil spill, pepper mill, pep pill, poison pill, quill, road kill, saw mill, **Spoonbill Cat**, T-bill, treadmill, **whippoorwill,** Will, windmill
Blue jay	ash tray, attaché, ballet, beret, bidet, bouquet, cabaret, cabernet, café, chalet, Chevrolet, croquet, flight pay, hair spray, **jay, manta ray, moray,** negligee, **Nene, osprey,** pepper spray, sleigh, **stingray,** subway, toupee, Valentine's day
Blue Whale	see **Airedale**
Boa	aloha, Mauna Loa
Boar	see **Albacore**
Bobcat	see **Alley Cat**
Boll weevil	nil
Bonito	see **Bronco**
Border Collie	Christmas holly, **Collie**, trolley, tea trolley
Brittany Spaniel	**Cocker spaniel, Springer spaniel**

Bronco

air show, art deco, backhoe, **bronco**, **buffalo**, bungalow, cash flow, cello, chapeau, chateau, crossbow, **crow**, **doe**, dog and pony show, domino, echo, escrow, free throw, gazebo, halo, hoe, inferno, longbow, mango, **minnow**, mistletoe, **mosquito**, oboe, Oleo, Oreo, peep show, piccolo, radio, rainbow, **rhino**, rodeo, scarecrow, ski tow, skid row, **sparrow**, standing O, stereo, tennis elbow, TKO, trousseau, volcano, widow

Brook Trout

bailout, boy scout, brown trout, cookout, cutthroat trout, dugout, cub scout, downspout, eagle scout, g**olden trout**, gout, lake trout, pitchout, rainbow trout, **rainout**, **sea trout,** **speckled trout**, strikeout,

Boxer

nil

Box Turtle

crepe myrtle, wax myrtle, loggerhead turtle, Ridley turtle, snapping turtle

Buck

beginner's luck, buzzard's luck, **duck**, dump truck, fire truck, hockey puck, ladder truck, pickup truck, sawbuck, tow truck, **woodchuck**

Buffalo

see **Bronco**

Bug

see **Bedbug**

Bull

pit bull, pull, steel wool, taffy pull

Bulldog

see **Bird Dog**

Bullfrog

see **Bulldog**

Bull Moose

abuse, caboose, calaboose, fruit juice, juice, masseuse, **goose**, **mongoose**, noose, papoose, produce, prune juice, **snow goose**

Bumblebee

see **Bee**

Bunny

dust bunny, funny money, honey, hush money, pin money

Burro

nil

Bushmaster   brew master, broadcaster, concertmaster, disaster, forecaster, mustard plaster, newscaster, sand blaster, sportscaster, toastmaster, quartermaster, telecaster, weathercaster

Butterfly   alibi, apple pie, barfly, battle cry, black eye, bolo tie, bow tie, buckeye, cow pie, deadeye, **dragonfly**, electric eye, FBI, **firefly**, gadfly, GI, hawk eye, hi-fi, jai-alai, lullaby, **magpie**, mai tai, necktie, pig sty, pinkeye, private eye, railroad tie, RBI, semi, string tie, tie dye, sty, **tsetse fly**, **walleye**

Buzzard   nil

Calf   carafe, cardiograph, decaf, flagstaff, gaffe, **giraffe**, hovercraft, phonograph, telegraph, sales staff

Calamari   actuary, adversary, beneficiary, Bloody Mary, **canary,** confectionary, coronary, dairy, dictionary, fairy, ferry, fiduciary, itinerary, judiciary, library, military, monastery, mortuary, **peccary,** secretary, Stradivari, sherry, stationary, tooth fairy

Calico Cat   see **Alley Cat**

Canadian Goose   **bull moose,** caboose, **mongoose, moose,** noose, papoose, snow goose, truce, abuse,

Camel   mammal, enamel

Canary   see **Calamari**

Capuchin Monkey   Chablis, church key, degree, fleur-de-lis, flunky, Frisbee, goatee, grease monkey, **howler monkey**, jamboree, junky, machete, **monkey**, pedigree, referee, renminbi, r**hesus monkey**, shoe tree, ski, s**pider monkey**, tee, tree.

Carrier Pigeon   clay pigeon, **homing pigeon**, **passenger pigeon**, religion, stool pigeon

Caribou   barbecue, brew, canoe, **cockatoo**, cork screw, **ewe**, **gnu**, hairdo, horse shoe, igloo, IOU, **kangaroo**, kazoo, micro brew, shampoo, tattoo, tofu, voodoo, Waterloo

Carp   autoharp, tarp, vibra harp

Cat	see **Alley Cat**
Caterpillar	distiller, driller, griller, killer, pain killer, Rototiller, weed killer
Catfish	see **Angelfish**
Cavalier King Charles Spaniel	see **Brittany Spaniel**
Centipede	bead, birdseed, chicken feed, duckweed, hayseed, **millipede**, nosebleed, poppy seed, screed, seaweed, stampede
Chamois	see **Bee**
Cheshire Cat	see **Alley Cat**
Cheetah	see **Akita**
Chick	chopstick, dipstick, **dik dik**, drumstick, gold brick, hat trick, ice pick, kick, lipstick, oil slick, pick, place kick, salt lick, sidekick, stick, **tick,** toothpick, yardstick, candlestick, pogo stick, swizzle stick
Chicken	awestricken, panic stricken, poverty stricken, **prairie chicken**, **spring chicken**
Chihuahua	nil
Chimpanzee	see **Bee**
Chinchilla	flotilla, **gorilla**, guerilla, hydrilla, sarsaparilla, villa
Chipmunk	bunk, drunk, junk, Podunk, **skunk**, slam dunk, steamer trunk, trunk
Clam	battering ram, cardiogram, exam, grand slam, hologram, **lamb**, monogram, mammogram, **ram**, scam, sky cam, spam, telegram, tinker's damn, traffic jam, web cam
Clydesdale	see **Airedale**
Cobra	nil

Cockatiel	automobile, bookmobile, buffing wheel, curb appeal, **eel**, **elephant seal**, Ferris wheel, flywheel, glockenspiel, **harp seal**, **leopard seal**, paddle wheel, **seal**, spinning wheel, stiletto heel
Cockatoo	see **Caribou**
Cocker Spaniel	see **Brittany Spaniel**
Cockroach	coach, poach, encroach, brooch, coach, **roach**, stagecoach
Cod	Cape Cod, divining rod, façade, firing squad, lightning rod, **scrod**, vice squad
Collie	see **Border Collie**
Colt	dead bolt, lag bolt, revolt, thunderbolt, toggle bolt
Condor	ambassador, cuspidor, door, humidor, **Labrador**, matador, picador
Coon	see **Baboon**
Copperhead	bedspread, blockhead, bobsled, bonehead, bread, bunk bed, cornbread, dogsled, featherbed, gingerbread, **hammerhead**, moped, rose bed, **steelhead** thoroughbred, tool shed, twin bed, water bed
Coral Snake	air brake, backache, bellyache, birthday cake, coffee break, disc brake, earthquake, emergency brake, fruitcake, grubstake, hand brake, **king snake**, parking brake, **rattlesnake**, **sea snake**, **snake,** snow flake, tax break
Cottonmouth	big mouth, motor-mouth.
Cottontail	see **Airdale**
Cougar	luger
Cow	chow, Dachau, frau, hausfrau, hoosegow, luau, plow, powwow, scow, snow plow
Coyote	see **Bee**

Crab	backstab, cab, crime lab, **fiddler crab**, gift of gab, **horseshoe crab**, **king crab**, science lab, space lab, taxicab
Crane	acid rain, aquaplane, airplane pane
Crawdad	Hot pad, hanging chad, undergrad, kneepad, launch pad, scratch pad, **shad,** shoulder pad.
Crayfish	see **Angelfish**
Cricket	parking ticket, pawn ticket, picket, ticket, speeding ticket, sticky wicket
Croc	acid rock, alarm clock, Bach, butcher-block, chopping block, cuckoo clock, dreadlock, flintlock, frock, grandfather clock, hemlock, padlock, **peacock,** penny stock, poppycock, punk rock, **Reebok**, shellshock, shock jock, shot clock, shuttlecock, smock, **springbok**, sweat sock, time clock, windsock, wok, **woodcock**
Crocodile	circular file, domicile, hair style, nail file, smile, sundial, turnstile
Crow	see **Bronco**
Cub	club, grub, nub, pub, sub, tub
Dachshund	[1] cummerbund, fund, refund [2] **bloodhound**, fairground, fogbound, foxhound, **greyhound**, muscle bound, playground, **wolfhound**.
Daddy Longlegs	nil
Dalmatian	adoration, annihilation, aggravation, animation, arbitration, asphyxiation, beautification, coeducation, constipation, contamination, coronation, corporation, decoration, detoxification, denigration, deodorization, depravation, desolation, dictation, education, electrification, elongation, gas station, hibernation, inebriation, insulation, litigation, sex education, space station, starvation, strangulation, taxation, transportation, vocation.
Damselfish	see **Angelfish**

Damsel Fly	see **Butterfly**
Deer	beer, boutonniere, brassiere, cauliflower ear, chandelier, charioteer, civil engineer, gondolier, headgear, landing gear, musketeer, peer, puppeteer, **reindeer** Shakespeare, spear, **steer, tapir**
Deerfly	see **Butterfly**
Deer Hound	see **Afghan Hound**
Deer Mouse	alehouse, beach house, blouse, bunkhouse, clubhouse, dog house, doll house, **dormouse, field mouse,** flophouse, **grouse,** guardhouse, hen house, jailhouse, lighthouse, **louse,** opera house, penthouse, slaughter house, smokehouse, statehouse, **titmouse**
Devilfish	see **Angelfish**
Diamond-back	backpack, blackjack, bootblack, bric-a-brac, Cadillac, cognac, gunnysack, hatchback, ice pack, gunny sack, hatchback, heart attack, kayak, knapsack, Muzak, Prozac, racetrack, **silverback**, racetrack, **razorback**, setback, six-pack, ski rack, smokestack, tarmac, thumbtack, tie rack
Dik-dik	see **chick**
Dingo	see **Black Widow**
Doberman	bedpan**,** caravan, caveman, congressman, doorman, **toucan**
Doe	see **Bronco**
Dog	see **Birddog**
Dolphin	bathtub gin, bobby pin, cave-in, clothespin, coonskin, cotton gin, dustbin, gin, hairpin, pigskin, Ritalin, rolling pin, safety pin, **sea urchin,** sheepskin, sloe gin, tenpin, violin
Donkey	Chablis, degree, fee, fleur-de-lis, goatee, Frisbee, jamboree, key, LSD, maitre d', pass key, pedigree, referee, renminbi, shoe tree, ski, tee, tree
Dormouse	see **Deer Mouse**

Dove	boxing glove, foxglove, golf glove, kid-glove, love, **mourning dove**, puppy love, white glove
Dover Sole	bankroll, beanpole, bedroll, bowl, charcoal, coal, goal, charcoal, cruise control, dust bowl, field goal, fishbowl, fishing pole, flag pole, **foal**, fox hole, hellhole, loophole, **mole**, opinion poll, patrol, payroll, peephole, pothole, rock and roll, ski patrol, ski pole, south pole, super bowl, toll, totem pole, washbowl
Draft Horse	see **Arabian Horse**
Dragonfly	see **Butterfly**
Drake	brake, cake, cheesecake, clambake, coffee break, cupcake, earthquake, fruitcake, **garter snake**, lake, rake, **rattlesnake**, **snake**, stomachache, tooth ache
Duck	see **Buck**
Duck-billed Platypus	**Octapus**
Duckling	king, **Ling**, ring, sling, string, swing, shoestring, teething ring
Dungeness Crab	see **Crab**
Eagle	see **Beagle**
Eaglet	bassinet, bayonet, briquette, cigarette, clarinet, coronet, Corvette, debt, dip net, ink-jet, jet, minuet, **mullet**, rocket, roulette, tea set, videocassette
Earthworm	see **Angleworm**
Eel	see **Cockatiel**
Egret	see **Eaglet**
Eland	Baby Grand, band, bandstand, brand, brass band, deckhand, Dixie land, grandstand, jug band, Krugerrand, quicksand, taxi stand
Electric Eel	see **Cockatiel**

Elephant	bunt, cold front, foxhunt, manhunt, scavenger hunt, witch hunt
Elephant Seal	see **Cockatiel**
Elk	nil
Elkhound	see **Afghan Hound**
Emperor penguin	bathtub gin, bobby pin, cave-in, clothespin, coonskin, cotton gin, dustbin, hairpin, pigskin, gin, Ritalin, rolling pin, sheepskin, tenpin, violin Berlin
Emu	see **Caribou**
Ermine	sermon, German, vermin
English Setter	chain letter, debtor, fan letter, go-getter, jet-setter, newsletter, pacesetter,
Eskimo Dog	see **Birddog**
Ewe	see **Caribou**
Falcon	nil
Fawn	biathlon, decathlon, Exxon, Freon, futon, icon, krypton, leprechaun, marathon, neon, peloton, **python**, **swan**, telethon, **toucan**, spawn, Yuan, zircon
Fer-de-lance	ambulance, barn dance, belly dance, break-dance, deodorants, finance, lap dance, romance, Saint Vitas' dance, stretch pants, sweatpants, tap dance, trance, underpants
Feral Hog	see **Birddog**
Ferret	carrot, claret, demerit, merit, parrot
Fiddler Crab	see **Crab**
Field Mouse	see **Deermouse**
Filly	nil

Finch	inch, cinch, pinch
Fire Ant	see **Ant**
Firefly	see **Butterfly**
Fish	see **Angelfish**
Fish Hawk	baby talk, cakewalk, catwalk, doubletalk, **hawk**, moonwalk, **night hawk**, pillow talk, shop talk, sleepwalk, space walk, tomahawk
Flamingo	see **Dingo**
Flea	see **Bee**
Flounder	nil
Fly	see **Butterfly**
Flying Fish	see **Angelfish**
Flying Squirrel	see **Black Squirrel**
Foal	**see Dover Sole**
Fox	see **Arctic Fox**
Fox Hound	see **Afghan Hound**
Fox Terrier	aircraft carrier, wind barrier, derriere
Frog	see **Birddog**
Fruit Fly	see **Butterfly**
Gamecock	see **Croc**
Gander	commander, coriander, belt sander, **salamander**
Gar	see **Alligator Gar**
Garter Snake	see **Coral Snake**

Gator	see **Alligator**
Gazelle	cartel, church bell, cowbell, detention cell, diving bell, fuel cell, hair jell, hotel, jail cell, motel, wishing well
Gecko	see **Black Widow**
Gerbil	see **Bluegill**
German Shepherd	**leopard**
Giant Panda	**Panda,** propaganda, veranda,
Giant Squid	see Captain Kidd, Madrid, power grid, skid, **squid**
Gila Monster	coiffeur, fur, liqueur, raconteur, saboteur, spur
Giraffe	see **Calf**
Glassfish	see **Angelfish**
Glowworm	see **Angleworm**
Gnat	see **Alley Cat**
Gnu	see **Caribou**
Goat	see **Angora Goat**
Golden Eagle	see **Beagle**
Golden Retriever	see **Beaver**
Golden Trout	see **Brook Trout**
Goldfinch	see **Finch**
Goldfish	see **Angelfish**
Goose	see **Bull Moose**
Gopher	chauffer, loafer

Gorilla	see **Chinchilla**
Gosling	see **Duckling**
Grackle	debacle, **jackal**, tackle, tabernacle debacle
Grasshopper	chopper, clodhopper, eavesdropper, eyedropper, flip flopper, hip hopper, sharecropper, teenybopper, topper
Gray Wolf	Beowulf, **gray wolf, red wolf, timber wolf**
Great Dane	see **Crane**
Great White Shark	see **Aardvark**
Green Snake	see **Coral Snake**
Green Turtle	see **Box Turtle**
Grey Fox	see **Fox**
Greyhound	see **Basset Hound**
Grizzly Bear	see **Bear**
Groundhog	see **Birddog**
Grouper	blooper, paratrooper, party-pooper, pooper-scooper, snooper, state trooper, storm trooper
Grouse	see **Deer Mouse**
Guide Dog	see **Birddog**
Guinea Hen	bullpen, fountain pen, **hen, peahen, wren b**ullpen, carcinogen, comedienne, den, five-and-ten, fox den, fountain pen, playpen, poison pen, RN, Zen, **wren**
Guinea Pig	bigwig, brig, gig, **guinea pig**, jury-rig, **pot-bellied pig**, powdered wig, shindig, sprig, trig, whirligig, wig
Guppy	**puppy, mud puppy**, yuppie

Gull	scull, **seagull**
Gypsy Moth	see **Moth**
Haddock	see **Croc**
Halibut	buzz cut, cigar butt, coconut, crew cut, haircut, lug nut, mutt, rotgut, scuttlebutt, short put, wing nut
Hammerhead	see **Copperhead**
Hamster	chauffeur, fur, liqueur, masseur, spur
Hard Shell Clam	see **Clam**
Hare	see **Bear**
Harp Seal	see **Cockatiel**
Hartebeest	see **Bee**
Hatchet Fish	see **Angelfish**
Hawk	see **Fish hawk**
Hedgehog	see **Birddog**
Heifer	nil
Hen	see **Guinea Hen**
Hermit Crab	see **Crab**
Herring	see **Gosling**
Heron	baron, robber baron
Hippo	Zippo
Hog	see **Birddog**
Hognose Snake	see **Coral Snake**

Holstein	assembly line, breadline, brine, bust line, carbine, chorus line, conga line, firing line, gold mine, grapevine, hot line, land mine, mine, moonshine, pine, pipeline, **porcupine**, punch line, salt mine, silver mine, shrine, sparkling wine, strip mine, **swine**, trap line, trotline, turbine, turpentine, valentine, wine
Homing Pigeon	see **Carrier Pigeon**
Honey Badger	nil
Honeybee	see **Bee**
Hoot Owl	see **Barn Owl**,
Horned toad	abode, area code, bar code, boatload, commode, dress code, Morse code, mother lode, payload, penal code, railroad, trainload, **tree toad**, wagon load, zip code
Hornet	nil
Horse	see **Arabian Horse**
Horsefly	see **Butterfly**
Horseshoe Crab	see **Crab**
Hound	see **Afghan Hound**
Howler Monkey	see **Capuchin Monkey**
Hummingbird	see **Bird**
Humpback Whale	see **Airdale**
Husky	see **Bee**
Hyena	arena, ballerina, cantina, **javelina**, marina, subpoena,
Ibex	duplex, hex, index, spandex, sex, Tex-Mex, texts, vex, wrecks
Ibis	bliss, hiss, kiss, miss, Swiss

Iguana	Americana, Botswana, fauna, marijuana, prima donna, Nirvana, sauna
Impala	Guatemala, Kampala, **koala**, Valhalla
Inchworm	see **Angleworm**
Insect	architect, benign neglect, defect, domino effect, halo effect, murder suspect, suspect
Irish Setter	see **English Setter**
Jackal	see **Grackle**
Jackass	see **Bass**
Jackrabbit	abbot, riding habit
Jaguar	see **Gar**
Jay	see **Blue Jay**
Javelina	see **Hyena**
Jellyfish	see **Angelfish**
June bug	see **Bug**
Kangaroo	see **Caribou**
Kangaroo Rat	see **Angora Cat**
Killer Bee	see **Bee**
Killer Whale	see **Airedale**
Komodo Dragon	bandwagon, battlewagon, chuck wagon, Conestoga wagon, covered wagon, paddy wagon, snapdragon, station wagon
King Cobra	nil
King Crab	see **Crab**

Kingfish	see **Angelfish**
King Fisher	nil
King Salmon	backgammon, famine
King Bird	see **Bird**
King Snake	see **Coral Snake**
King Vulture	see **Black Vulture**
Kit Fox	see **Fox**
Kitten	Britton, flea-bitten, mitten, snake-bitten
Kiwi	see **Bee**
Koala	see **Impala**
Kodiak	see **Diamondback**
Koi	boy, busboy, cowboy, decoy, poi, envoy, ploy, tinker toy
Krill	see **Bluegill**
Labrador	see **Boar**
Ladybug	see **Bug**
Lake Trout	bailout, beat out, black out, blot out, **brook trout**, burnout, buyout, cop out, Cub Scout, devout, downspout, drought, Eagle Scout, gout, dugout, flameout, Girl Scout, knockout, lookout, phase out, **speckled trout**, talent scout, **trout**
Lamb	see **Clam**
Lamprey	see **Bee**
Lap Dog	see **Birddog**
Largemouth Bass	see **Ass**
Lark	see **Aardvark**

Leech   beech, breach, bleach, each, speech, impeach, Long Beach, Palm Beach, Myrtle Beach, Newport Beach, Daytona Beach, Huntington Beach, Miami Beach, Omaha Beach, peach, Virginia Beach

Leghorn   see **Bighorn**

Lemming   bullring, G-string, hamstring, shoestring, sing sing, sling, teething ring.

Lemon Shark   see **Aardvark**

Lemon Sole   see **Dover Sole**

Lemur   creamer, femur, reamer, schemer, screamer, steamer, streamer, blasphemer, daydreamer, redeemer

Leopard   Shepherd

Leopard Seal   see **Cockatiel**

Lhasa Apso   nil

Lice   **mice**, sacrifice, thin ice

Lightning Bug   see **Bug**

Ling   see **Gosling**

Lion   Hawaiian, Paraguayan, Uruguayan, scion

Lion fish   see **Angelfish**

Lipizzaner   medal of honor

Lizard   see **Alligator Lizard**

Llama   Brahma, drama, mama, Bahama, pajama, Dalai Lama, docudrama, melodrama, panorama, photodrama, psychodrama, Yokohama

Lobster   mobster

Locust   blind trust, wanderlust

Loggerhead Turtle	see **Box Turtle**
Longhorn	see **Bighorn**
Loon	see **Baboon**
Louse	see **Deer Mouse**
Love Bird	see **Bird**
Lynx	drinks, jinx
Macaw	Arkansas, attorney at law, band saw, bear claw, blue law, brother-in-law, buzz saw, bylaw, chaw, chainsaw, civil law, claw, coleslaw, coping saw, daughter-in-law, father-in-law, flaw, jaw, jigsaw, keyhole saw, law, lockjaw, Mackinac, mother-in-law, Murphy's Law, Omaha, Panama, paw, raw, ripsaw, saber saw, Saginaw, scofflaw, seesaw, Shah, son-in-law, southpaw, straw, squaw, Utah, whipsaw, Wichita
Mackerel	horse mackerel, king mackerel
Maggot	aeronaut, astronaut,
Magpie	see **Butterfly**
Mako Shark	see **Aardvark**
Malamute	birthday suit, boot, cheroot, crapshoot, deaf mute, flute, galoot, G suit, hip boot, jumpsuit, leisure suit, pantsuit, parachute, snowsuit, spacesuit, sweat suit, swim suit, track suit, trade route, zootsuit,
Mallard	backyard, bard, barnyard, blowhard, bodyguard, bone yard, business card, Christmas card, color guard, credit card, farmyard, graveyard, honor guard, ID card, junkyard, leotard, lifeguard, petard, scorecard, video card, wild card
Mamba	samba, mamba, viola da gamba
Manatee	see **Bee**
Man-o-war	see **Boar**

Manta ray — see **Blue jay**

Manx Cat — see **Angora Cat**

Mare — see **Bear**

Marlin — see **Emperor Penguin**

Marmoset — barrette, chess set, cigarette, clarinet, cold sweat, coronet, Corvette, fish net, jet set, roulette – base hit, drill bit, snake pit, stock split, tar pit, tourniquet

Martin — bathtub gin, bin, bobby pin, cavein, chin, clothespin, coonskin, cotton gin, drive in, fin, firing pin, gin, hairpin, grin, looney bin, pigskin, safety pin, **Simian**, sin, spin, tin, violin

Maverick — see **Chick**

Mayfly — see **Butterfly**

Meadowlark — see **Aardvark**

Meer Kat — see **Alley Cat**

Milk Snake — see **Coral Snake**

Millipede — see **Centipede**

Mink — cuff link, drink, ice rink, ink, kitchen sink, mixed drink, red ink, rinky-dink, shrink, sink

Minnow — see **Bronco**

Mockingbird — see **Bird**

Mole — see **Foal**

Monarch Butterfly — see **Butterfly**

Mongoose — see **Canadian Goose**

Mongrel — nil

Monkey	**see Capuchin Monkey**
Moose	see B**ull Moose**
Moray Eel	see **Cockatiel**
Mosquito	see **Bronco**
Mosquito Hawk	see **Fish Hawk**
Moth	broth, breechcloth, cloth, drop cloth, face cloth, loincloth, **sloth**, tablecloth, washcloth
Mountain Goat	see **Angora Goat**
Mountain lion	see **Lion**
Mourning Dove	see **Dove**
Mouse	see **Deermouse**
Mudpuppy	see **Guppy**
Mule	barstool, carpool, cathouse, correspondence school, fool, footstool, fuel, school, grade school, grammar school, home school, Liverpool, medical school, motor pool, nursery school, parochial school, reform school, senior high school, summer school, synfuel, toadstool, tire tool, van pool, vestibule, whirlpool
Mule Deer	**Deer**
Mullet	see **Eaglet**
Musk ox	see **Fox**
Muskrat	see **Alley Cat**
Musky	see **Husky**
Mussel	bustle
Mustang	boomerang, chain gang, fang, gang, road gang

Myna Bird   see **Bird**

Nanny goat   see **Billy Goat**

Needlefish   see **Angelfish**

Nene   see **Blue Jay**

Neon Tetra   baccarat, chutzpah, et cetera, spa,

Newt   see **Malamute**

Night crawler   basketballer, brawler, fireballer, footballer, hauler, knuckleballer, mauler, pub crawler, stonewaller, squalor, trawler

Night hawk   see **Fish Hawk**

Nightingale   see **Airedale**

Northern Pike   dirt bike, exercise bike, hunger strike, mini bike, mountain bike, tax hike, thunder strike, trail bike, turnpike

Nutria   **Tilapia**

Ocelot   aquanaut, astronaut, big shot, blind spot, blood clot, blot, buckshot, chamber pot, cheap shot, clot, coffeepot, cosmonaut, cot, despot, dreadnaught, dunk shot, feedlot, fox-trot, gunshot, jackpot, juggernaut, knot, mascot, melting pot, moon shot, mug shot, parking lot, patriot, penalty shot, polka dot, pot, robot, slap shot, slingshot, slipknot, sunspot, teapot, tot, touch-me-not, turkey trot, yacht

Octopus   glamour-puss, platypus, puss, schuss, sourpuss

Old English Sheepdog   see **Birddog**

Opossum   blossom

Orangutan   [1] afghan, anchorman, ape-man, bedpan, clan, fan, frogman, family man, frying pan, hatchet man, Iran, Japan, mailman, newsman, oilcan, oilman, ombudsman, Piltdown man, plan, sampan, saucepan, snowman, superman [2] see **Mustang**

Orca   nil

Oriole   see **Mole**

Osprey   see **Blue Jay**

Ostrich   bait and switch, drainage ditch, fast-pitch, jock itch, kitsch, perfect pitch, rich, sales pitch, slow-pitch, snitch, switch, timber hitch, toggle switch, witch, wild pitch

Otter   alma mater, blotter, boycotter, firewater, flyswatter, globe-trotter, groundwater, hot water, ice water, rainwater, saltwater, **sea otter**, soda water, squatter, tap water, teeter-totter, wastewater, whitewater

Owl   see **Barn Owl**

Owlet   see **Eaglet**

Ox   see **Fox**

Oyster   nil

Packrat   see **Alley Cat**

Palomino   Angelino, bambino, cappuccino, casino, concertino

Panda   memoranda, propaganda, Uganda, veranda

Panther   nil

Parakeet   aquavit, athlete, beet, bed sheet, biathlete, box seat, cheat, cheat sheet, cold feet, crib sheet, deadbeat, decathlete, drumbeat, easy street, elite, hot seat, jump seat, potty seat, prickly heat, pink sheet, rap sheet, retreat, skeet, spreadsheet, suite, swap meet, Wall Street

Parrot   see **Ferret**

Partridge   auction bridge, bridge, contract bridge, footbridge, ridge, fridge, suspension bridge

Passenger Pigeon   see **Carrier Pigeon**

Peacock	see **Croc**
Peahen	see **Guinea Hen**
Peccary	see **Calimari**
Pekinese	breeze, **bumblebees**, artilleries, bikinis, Chablis, **chamois**, cheese, **chimpanzees**, Chinese, Christmas trees, church keys, college degrees, daiquiris, epees, factories, fees, Ferraris, fleur-de-lis, Frisbees, goatees, golf tees, grease monkeys, green fees, hemlock trees, hibachis, **honeybees**, **huskies**, jamborees, Japanese, **killer bees**, **kiwis**, law degrees, lingerie's, machetes, Maitre Ds', **manatees**, martinis, pass keys, pedigrees, privies, referees, rotisseries, shoe trees, skeleton keys, snow skis, tepees
Pelican	bullpen, comedienne, den, five-and-ten, fountain pen, playpen, poison pen, RN
Penguin	see **Emperor Penguin**
Perch	church, research, strip search.
Peregrine	see **Dolphin**
Persian cat	see **Alley Cat**
Pheasant	birthday present, present
Pickerel	see **Bluegill**
Pig	see **Guinea Pig**
Pigeon	see **Carrier Pigeon**
Piglet	see **Marmoset**
Pike	see **Northern Pike**
Pileated	
Woodpecker	**red billed, red breasted woodpecker, red headed woodpecker, pileated woodpecker**

Pilot Fish	see Angelfish
Pilot Whale	see **Airedale**
Pinto	see **Bronco**
Piranha	Botswana, fauna, prima donna, Americana
Pit Bull	see **Bull**
Polar bear	see **Bear**
Polecat	see **Alley Cat**
Pollywog	see **Birddog**
Polo Pony	see **Abalone**
Pomeranian	Albanian, Jordanian, Lithuanian, Panamanian, Pennsylvanian, Tanzanian, Ukrainian
Pompano	piano, soprano
Pony	see **Abalone**
Poodle	apple strudel, doodle, kit and caboodle
Porcupine	**see Holstein**
Porpoise	nil
Possum	see **Black Drum**
Pot-bellied Pig	see **Guinea Pig**
Prairie Chicken	see **Chicken**
Prairie Dog	see **Birddog**
Prawn	see **Fawn**
Praying Mantis	Atlantis

Pronghorn	see **Bighorn**
Puff adder	extension ladder, fish ladder, step ladder
Puffer Fish	see **Angelfish**
Puffin	muffin
Pug	see **Bug**
Pullet	see **Eaglet**
Puma	Montezuma
Puppy	see **Guppy**
Purple Finch	see **Finch**
Pygmy Goat	see **Angora goat**
Pygmy Owl	see **Barn Owl**
Pygmy Whale	see **Airedale**
Python	see **Prawn**
Quahog	see **Birddog**
Quail	see **Airedale**
Quarter Horse	see **Horse**
Quetzal	cabal, canal, corral, decal
Rabbit	abbot, cohabit, habit
Raccoon	see **Baboon**
Racehorse	see **Arabian Horse**
Rainbow Trout	see **Brook Trout**
Ram	see **Clam**

Raptor	see **Albacore**
Rat	see **Alley Cat**
Rat Snake	see **Coral Snake**
Rattlesnake	see **Coral Snake**
Raven	bull pen, carcinogen, cayenne, comedienne, den, five and ten, fountain pen, men, playpen, poison pen, RN
Razorback	see **Diamondback**
Red Ant	see **Ant**
Red Billed Woodpecker	see **Woodpecker**
Redbird	see **Bird**
Red Breasted Woodpecker	see **Woodpecker**
Redfish	see **Angelfish**
Red Fox	see **Fox**
Redheaded Woodpecker	see **Woodpecker**
Red Panda	see **Giant Panda**
Red Snapper	boot strapper, catnapper, dognapper, flapper, gangsta rapper, kidnapper, scrapper, trapper, whippersnapper, wire tapper, wrapper
Red Wolf	see **Gray Wolf**
Reebok	see **Croc**
Reef Shark	see **Aardvark**
Reindeer	see **Deer**

Rhesus Monkey	see **Capuchin Monkey**
Rhino	see **Bronco**
Ribbon Fish	see **Angelfish**
Ridley Turtle	see **Box Turtle**
River Otter	see **Otter**
Roadrunner	rumrunner
Robin	see **Dolphin**
Rock Bass	see **ass**
Rockfish	see **Angelfish**
Rock Lobster	see **Lobster**
Rodent	cement, convent, detent, pup tent, regiment, rubber cement, vice president
Rooster	see **Bantam Rooster**
Rottweiler	nil
Saber Toothed Tiger	**Bengal Tiger, Siberian tiger**
Sable	cable, fable, gale, label, round table, stable, table, timetable, turntable
Sailfish	see **Angelfish**
Saint Bernard	armed guard, bankcard, body guard, green card, shin guard
Salamander	see **Gander**
Salmon	see **Atlantic Salmon**
Sand Dollar	collar, flea collar, white-collar

Sand Fly	see **Butterfly**
Sand Hill Crane	see **Great Dane**
Sandpiper	chauffeur, entrepreneur, restaurateur, saboteur, spur
Sardine	acetylene, caffeine, canteen, e-zine, gangrene, guillotine, Halloween, latrine, limousine, magazine, marine, morpheme, nicotine, pinball machine, putting green, queen, ravine, screen, slot machine, smokescreen, spleen, submarine, trampoline, Vaseline, washing machine, **wolverine**
Savannah Cat	see **Alley Cat**
Sawfish	see **Angelfish**
Scallop	nil
Schnauzer	carouser, rabble rouser, trouser, web browser
Schnook	coloring book, comic book, fry cook, pastry cook, telephone book
Scorpion	nil
Scotty	see **Bee**
Screech Owl	see **Barn Owl**
Scrod	see **Cod**
Sea anemone	nil
Sea Bass	see **Ass**
Sea Cow	see **Cow** (no pun intended)
Sea Eagle	see **Beagle**
Seagull	see **Gull**
Sea Hawk	see **Fish Hawk**

Seahorse	see **Arabian Horse**
Seal	see **Cockatiel**
Sea Lion	see **Lion** (no pun intended)
Sea Slug	see **Bedbug**
Sea Snake	see **Coral Snake**
Sea otter	see **Otter**
Sea Trout	see **Brook Trout**
Seahorse	see **Arabian Horse**
Sea Urchin	see **Dolphin**
Seeing Eye Dog	see **Birddog**
Shad	see **Crawdad**
Shark	see **Aardvark**
Sheep	barkeep, chimney sweep, creep, jeep, rubbish heap, scrap heap, sleep, trash heap, veep
Sheep Dog	see **Birddog**
Shellfish	see **Angelfish**
Sheltie	see **Bee**
Shetland Pony	see **Abalone**
Shetland Sheepdog	see **Birddog**
Shrew	see **Caribou**
Shrimp	blimp, imp, wimp
Siamese Cat	see **Angora Cat**

Siberian Tiger	**Bengal Tiger, Siberian tiger**
Sidewinder	binder, coffee grinder, fact finder, meat grinder, organ grinder
Silkworm	see **Angleworm**
Silverback	see **Diamondback**
Silver Fox	see **Fox**
Simian	see **Martin**
Skunk	see **Chipmunk**
Skylark	see **Aardvark**
Sled Dog	see **Birddog**
Sloth	see **Moth**
Slug	see **Bedbug**
Smelt	conveyor belt, corn belt, fan belt, garter belt, money belt, seat belt
Snail	see **Airedale**
Snail Darter	barter, charter, garter, kick-starter
Snake	see **Coral Snake**
Snapping Turtle	see **Box Turtle**
Snipe	bagpipe, hype, pitch pipe, stovepipe, tailpipe
Snow Goose	see **Canadian Goose**
Snow Leopard	peppered, shepherd
Snowshoe Hare	see **Bear**
Snowy Owl	see **Barn Owl**

Sockeye	see **Firefly**
Sow	see **Cow**
Sparrow	see **Bronco**
Speckled Trout	see **Trout**
Sperm Whale	see **Airedale**
Spider	see **Black Widow Spider**
Spider Monkey	see **Capuchin Monkey**
Springbok	see **Croc**
Springer Spaniel	see **Brittany Spaniel**
Spoonbill Cat	see **Angora Cat**
Spring Chicken	see **Chicken**
Sphynx Cat	see **Angora Cat**
Spoonbill Cat	see **Ally Cat**
Squid	see **Giant Squid**
Squirrel	see **Black Squirrel**
Stag	beanbag, body bag, doggie bag, dog tag, flag, jet lag, price tag, punching bag, saddle bag, sandbag, toe-tag, tote bag
Stallion	battalion, Italian, medallion
Starfish	see **Angelfish**
Starling	apron string, bee sting, boxing ring, engagement ring, nose ring, teething ring, wedding ring
Steelhead	see **Copperhead**
Steenbok	see **Croc**

Steer	see **Deer**
Stinkbug	see **Bedbug**
Stingray	see **Blue jay**
Stork	cork, fork, New York, pitchfork, salad fork, tuning fork
Sturgeon	brain surgeon, plastic surgeon, surgeon, virgin
Sunfish	see **Angelfish**
Swallow	Apollo, Sao Paulo
Swan	see **Prawn**
Swine	see **Porcupine**
Swordfish	see **Angelfish**
Tabby Cat	see **Angora Cat**
Tadpole	see **Foal**
Tapeworm	see **Angleworm**
Tapir	see **Deer**
Tarantula	nil
Tarpon	see **Atlantic Salmon**
Tasmanian Devil	bevel, bi-level, carpenter's level, daredevil, dishevel, entry-level, level, sea level, split level, water level
Teal	see **Cockatiel**
Termite	bagpipe, blight, bombsight, box kite, bullfight, campsite, cellulite, cockfight, cockfight, dogfight, dynamite, firefight, flashlight, fleabite, floodlight, frostbite, gunfight, headlight, kite, lamplight, limelight, meteorite, moonlight, overbite, parasite, penlight, pilot light, prizefight, satellite, searchlight, skylight, spaceflight, spotlight, stalagmite, stalactite, traffic light, torchlight, web site

Terrapin	see **Dolphin**
Tic	see **Chick**
Tiger	see **Bengal Tiger, Siberian tiger**
Tiger Shark	see **Aardvark**
Tiger Shrimp	see **Shrimp**
Tilapia	see **Nutria**
Timber Wolf	see **Gray Wolf**
Titmouse	see **Deer Mouse**
Toad	see **Horned Toad**
Tomcat	see **Alley Cat**
Tortoise	see **Ibis**
Toucan	see **Doberman**
Toy Fox Terrier	see **Fox Terrier**
Triggerfish	see **Angelfish**
Tree Frog	see **Birddog**
Tree Swallow	see **Swallow**
Tree Toad	see **Horned Toad**
Trout	see **Lake Trout**
Trumpeter Swan	see **Fawn**
Tsetse Fly	see **Butterfly**
Tuna	Kaduna, Montezuma, **vicuna**,
Turkey	see **Bee**

Turkey Buzzard	**Buzzard**
Turkey Vulture	see **Black Vulture**
Turtle	see **Box Turtle**
Turtle dove	see **Dove**
Vampire Bat	see **Angora Cat**
Vampire Squid	**see Giant Squid**
Varmint	blueprint, fingerprint, lint, mint, newsprint, skinflint, wind sprint
Vicuna	see **Tuna**
Viper	bagpiper, diaper, sniper
Vole	see **Foal**
Vulture	see **Black Vulture**
Wallaby	see **Bee**
Walleye	see **Butterfly**
Walrus	airbus, blunderbuss, bus, minibus, school bus, surplus
Wapiti	Atlantic City, Carson City, city, committee, Dodge City, kitty, Mexico City, New York City, Panama City, Rapid City, Salt Lake City, self-pity, Sioux City
Warthog	see **Birddog**
Wasp	nil
Watchdog	see **Birddog**
Water Beetle	nil
Water Buck	see **Buck**

Water Buffalo	see **Bronco**
Water Moccasin	**see Dolphin**
Weasel	easel, diesel, measles
Weevil	upheaval
Whale	see **Airedale**
Whippet	banana split, bit, cockpit, culprit, counterfeit, grit, hypocrite, obit, pulpit, tar pit, snake pit
Whip-poor-Will	see **Bluegill**
White Bass	see **Ass**
Whitefish	see **Angelfish**
White Tailed Deer	see **Deer**
Whiting	see **Herring**
Whooping Crane	see **Great Dane**
Wild Boar	see **Albacore**
Wildcat	see **Alley Cat**
Wirehaired Terrier	see **Fox Terrier**
Wildebeest	far east, feast, middle east, northeast, yeast
Wolf	see **Gray Wolf**
Wolfhound	see **Afghan Hound**
Wolf pack	**see Diamondback**
Wolverine	see **Sardine**
Wombat	see **Alley Cat**

Woodchuck	see **Buck**
Woodcock	see **Croc**
Wood Duck	see **Buck**
Woodpecker	double-decker, exchequer, fact-checker, rubbernecker, wrecker
Wood pussy	nil
Worm	see **Angleworm**
Wren	see **Guinea Hen**
Yak	**see Diamondback**
Yellow-Bellied Sapsucker	Bib and Tucker
Yellow Jacket	numbers racket, pay packet, racquet, squash racket, tennis racket
Yellow Lab	**Black Lab**
Yorkshire Terrier	see **Fox Terrier**
Zebra	nil
Zebra Fish	see **Angelfish**
Zebra Mule	see **Mule**

APPENDIX C
ADVERB HERD

Adverb: how, when, where and to what degree

— A —

Aback
Abaft
Abashedly
Abeam
Abed

Abhorrently
Abjectly
Ably
Abnormally
Aboard

Abominably
About
Above
Above all
Aboveground

Abreast
Abroad
Abruptly
Absently
Absentmindedly

Absolutely
Abstractly
Acoustically
Acridly
Across

Actively
Actually
Acutely
Adagio
Additionally

Afield
Afire
Aflame
Afloat
Aflutter

Afoot
Afore
Afoul
Afresh
Aft

After
After all
Afterwards
Again
Agape

Aggressively
Agilely
Agleam
Aglitter
Aglow

Ago
Agonizingly
Agreeably
Agriculturally
Aground

Ahead
Aimlessly
Airily
Ajar
Akimbo

Along with
Alongshore
Alongside
Aloof
Aloud

Already
Alright
Also
Alternately
Altogether

Altruism
Altruistically
Always
Amazingly
Ambiguously

Ambitiously
Amenable
Amenably
Amiably
Amiss

Amok
Amuck
Analogously
Analytically
Andante

Anew
Angelically
Angrily
Animatedly
Annoyingly

Anywhere
Apart
Apathetically
Apiece
Apolitically

Apologetically
Apparently
Appreciably
Appreciatively
Approaching

Appropriately
Approvingly
Approximately
Apropos
Aptly

Arbitrarily
Archaeologically
Architecturally
Ardently
Arduously

Arduously
Aromatically
Around
Arrogantly
Articulately

Artificially
Artistically
Artlessly
As a rule
Asexually

Astride
Astronomically
Asunder
At once
At times

Athletically
Athwart
Atilt
Atonally
Atop

Atrociously
Attentively
Attributively
Audaciously
Audibly

Augustly
Auspiciously
Austerely
Authentically
Authoritatively

Automatically
Autonomously
Avariciously
Avidly
Avoidably

Avowedly
Awash
Away
Awesomely
Awfully

Adeptly	Alertly	Artfully	Ashamedly	Awhile
Adequately	Alfresco	Annually	Ashore	Awkwardly
Adjacently	Alias	Anon	Aside	Awry
Admirably	Alike	Anonymously	Aside from	Accumulate
Admittedly	All	Antagonistically	Askance	Accuse
Adorably	All out	Antecedently	Askew	Admit
Adrift	All right	Antiseptically	Aslant	Aggrandize
Advance	Allegorically	Antithetically	Asleep	Agitate
Adventurously	Allegretto	Anxious	Assertively	Amass
Adversely	All-fired	Anxiously	Assiduously	Amplify
Advisably	All-round	Anyhow	Assiduously	Anger
Aerodynamically	Allusively	Anymore	Assuredly	Annoy
Afar	Almost	Anyplace	Astern	Assimilate
Affably	Aloft	Anytime	Astir	Assist
Affectionately	Alone	Anyway	Astray	Augment
Affluently	Along			

— B —

Back	Before	Betwixt	Boastfully	Broadmindedly
Backhand	Before now	Bewilderingly	Blithely	Broadside
Backhanded	Beforehand	Beyond	Bloodily	Brokenly
Backstage	Begrudgingly	Biannually	Bloodlessly	Brutally
Backward	Behind	Biennially	Bodily	Brutishly
Badly	Behindhand	Big time	Boisterously	Bucolically
Baldly	Belatedly	Bigheartedly	Boldly	Bumptiously
Banally	Belligerently	Bimonthly	Bombastically	Bunglingly
Banteringly	Below	Bitingly	Boorishly	Bureaucratically
Barbarously	Beneath	Bitterly	Bounteously	Busily
Bareback	Beneficially	Biweekly	Bravely	But
Barefoot	Benevolently	Blamably	Brazenly	By all means
Barehanded	Benignantly	Blamelessly	Breathlessly	By and large
Barelegged	Benignly	Blandly	Breezily	By chance
Barely	Berserk	Blankly	Briefly	By now
Bashfully	Beseechingly	Bleakly	Brightly	By the way
Basely	Besides	Blessedly	Brilliantly	Byronically
Bearishly	Best	Blindly	Briskly	Boost
Beauteously	Betimes	Blissfully	Broadly	Burden
Beautifully				

— C —

Caddishly	Chidingly	Colossally	Constantly	Cowardly
Cagily	Chiefly	Comfortably	Constitutionally	Coyly
Calculatedly	Childishly	Comically	Consummately	Cozily
Callously	Chivalrously	Commendably	Contemporaneously	Crabbily
Callow	Chromatically	Commercially	Contemptibly	Craftily
Calmly	Chronically	Commonly	Contentedly	Crankily
Candidly	Circa	Communally	Contentiously	Crassly
Cannily	Circuitously	Compactly	Continually	Cravenly
Cantankerously	Circumspectly	Comparably	Continuously	Crazily
Capably	Circumstantially	Comparatively	Contra	Creakily
Capaciously	Clandestinely	Compassionately	Contractually	Creatively
Capriciously	Clannishly	Compatibly	Contrariwise	Credibly
Cardinal	Classically	Compellingly	Contrary	Creditably
Carefully	Clean	Competently	Contritely	Credulously
Carelessly	Clearly	Completely	Conveniently	Creepily
Carefully	Clemently	Comprehensively	Conventionally	Criminally
Carelessly	Cleverly	Compulsively	Conversationally	Crisply
Carnally	Clinically	Concomitantly	Conversely	Crisscross
Casually	Cliquishly	Concretely	Convincingly	Critically
Categorically	Clockwise	Concretively	Convivially	Cross country
Caustically	Closely	Condescendingly	Coolly	Crossways
Cautiously	Clumsily	Conditionally	Correspondingly	Crosswise
Cavalierly	Coarsely	Confessedly	Coolly	Crucially
Central	Coaxingly	Confidently	Correspondingly	Crudely
Centrally	Cockamamie	Congenially	Copiously	Cruelly
Ceremoniously	Cockeyed	Congruently	Cordially	Curiously
Certainly	Coequally	Congruously	Correctly	Culpably
Characteristically	Coherently	Conscientiously	Corrosively	Culturally
Charitably	Coincidentally	Consciously	Corruptly	Cunningly
Charmingly	Coincidently	Consecutively	Cosmetically	Curiously
Chastely	Cold-bloodedly	Consequently	Counter	Currently
Chauvinistically	Coldly	Conservatively	Country-wide	Cursorily
Cheerfully	Collect	Considerably	Courageously	Curtly
Cheerily	Collectively	Considerately	Courageously	Customarily
Chemically	Colorfully	Consistently	Courteously	Cuttingly
Cherubically	Colorlessly	Conspicuously	Covertly	Cynically

— D —

Daily	Defiantly	Desperately	Dishonestly	Downhill
Daintily	Dejectedly	Despitefully	Dispassionately	Downright
Damnably	Delectably	Despondently	Dispiritedly	Downstage
Damned	Deliberately	Destructively	Distantly	Downstairs
Dangerously	Delicately	Desultorily	Distinct	Downstate
Darkly	Deliciously	Determinedly	Distinctively	Downstream
Darn	Delightedly	Devotedly	Distressingly	Downtown
Dashingly	Delightfully	Devoutly	Disturbing	Downward
Dauntlessly	Delinquently	Diagonally	Diversely	Dramatically
Dazedly	Deliriously	Differently	Divinely	Dreadfully
Dead	Deluxe	Diffusely	Divisively	Dreamily
Deadly	Democratically	Diligently	Dogmatically	Drearily
Deadpan	Demonically	Dimly	Dolefully	Drolly
Dearly	Demonstrably	Diplomatically	Dolorously	Drowsily
Debonairly	Demurely	Direct	Dominantly	Dryly
Deceitfully	Densely	Directly	Doubly	Dubiously
Deceivingly	Dependably	Dirt-cheap	Doubtfully	Due
Decidedly	Depraved	Disagreeably	Doubtingly	Dully
Decisively	Derisively	Disapprovingly	Doubtless	Dumbly
Decorously	Derogatorily	Disastrous	Doubtlessly	Durably
Deeply	Designedly	Disconsolately	Dowdily	Dutifully
Defensively	Desirably	Discreetly	Down	Dynamically

— E —

Eagerly	Effortlessly	Endways	Essentially	Exclusively
Earlier	Effusively	Energetically	Eternally	Exhaustively
Early	Egocentrically	Engagingly	Ethereally	Exotically
Earnestly	Egotistically	Enormously	Ethnically	Expansively
Earthward	Egregiously	Ensuing	Eugenically	Expectantly
Easily	Either	Enthusiastically	Evasively	Expeditiously
East	Elaborately	Enviously	Even	Experimental
Easy	Electrically	Epidemically	Eventually	Expertly
Eccentrically	Electronically	Episodically	Evidently	Explosively
Economically	Elegantly	Equably	Ever	Expressively
Ecstatically	Elliptically	Equally	Everlasting	Extemporaneously
Ecumenically	Eloquently	Equitably	Evermore	Extensively
Edgeways	Else	Equivocally	Everywhere	Externally
Edgewise	Elsewhere	Erectly	Exactly	Extra
Editorially	Emotionally	Ergo	Exceedingly	Extraneously

Eerily	Emphatically	Erratically	Excellently	Extreme
Effectively	Empirically	Erroneously	Exceptionally	Extremely
Effetely	En masse	Erstwhile	Excessively	Extrinsically
Efficaciously	Endearing	Especially	Excitedly	Exuberantly
Efficiently				

— F —

Fabulously	Faultily	Fitfully	Fore	Freely
Facetiously	Faultlessly	Fittingly	Foremost	Frenetically
Face-to-face	Favorably	Fixedly	Forever	Frequently
Facilely	Fearfully	Flabbily	Forgivingly	Frenzied
Faintly	Feasibly	Flagrantly	Forlornly	Fretfully
Faithfully	Fecklessly	Flamboyantly	Formally	Friendly
Faithlessly	Feebly	Flaming	Forsooth	Frightfully
Fallaciously	Ferociously	Flatly	Forth	Frigidly
Fallibly	Fervently	Flatteringly	Forthright	Frivolously
Familiarly	Festively	Flauntingly	Fortunately	Front
Famously	Feverishly	Fleetingly	Forward	Frontward
Fanatically	Fictively	Flimsily	Foully	Frugally
Fancifully	Fierce	Flippantly	Foursquare	Fruitlessly
Fancily	Fiercely	Fluently	Fourth	Fugitively
Fantastically	Figuratively	Fluidly	Fractiously	Full bore
Far	Finally	Following	Fragrantly	Fully
Farther	Financially	Fondly	Frailly	Fundamentally
Fast	Finely	Foolishly	Frankly	Furiously
Fastidiously	Firmly	Foppishly	Frantically	Further
Fatalistically	First	Forbiddingly	Fraudulently	Furthermore
Fatally	Firsthand	Forcefully	Freakishly	Future
Fatuously	Fiscally	Forcibly		

— G —

Gaily	Genetically	Gladly	Good-naturedly	Greatly
Gainfully	Genially	Glaringly	Gracefully	Greedily
Gallantly	Genteelly	Gleefully	Graciously	Grievously
Gamely	Gentility	Glibly	Gradually	Grimly
Garishly	Gently	Globally	Grammatically	Groggily
Garrulously	Geographically	Gloomily	Grandiloquently	Grossly
Gaudily	Geologically	Gloriously	Grandly	Grotesquely
Gawkily	Ghoulishly	Glumly	Graphically	Grudgingly
Generally	Giddily	Gluttonously	Gratefully	Gruffly
Generically	Gingerly	Good-heartedly	Gratuitously	Guardedly
Generously	Gladly	Good-humoredly	Gravely	Gymnastically

—H—

Habitually	Haughtily	Helter-skelter	Highhandedly	Hourly
Half-and-half	Headfirst	Hence	Highly	Hungrily
Half-heartedly	Headlong	Henceforth	High-mindedly	However
Halfway	Head-on	Here	Hilariously	Howsoever
Handily	Healthily	Hereabout	Historically	Hugely
Haphazardly	Heartedly	Hereafter	Hither	Humanely
Happily	Heartily	Hereby	Hoarsely	Humanly
Hard	Heartlessly	Herein	Holistically	Humbly
Hard-heartedly	Heatedly	Hereof	Homeward	Humorously
Hardly	Heavily	Heretofore	Honestly	Hundredfold
Hardy	Heretically	Hereupon	Honorably	Hurriedly
Harmlessly	Hectically	Herewith	Hopefully	Hurtfully
Harmoniously	Heedlessly	Heroically	Hopelessly	Hygienically
Harmonizing	Heinously	Hesitantly	Horribly	Hypnotically
Harshly	Hellishly	High	Hospitably	Hypothetically
Hastily	Helpfully	Higher	Hotly	Hysterically
Hatefully				

—I—

Icily	Impossibly	Indecently	Inherently	Intently
Identically	Impotently	Indecisively	Inhumanely	Interestingly
Idiotic	Imprecisely	Indeed	Initially	Inwardly
Idiotically	Impressively	Indefatigably	Inland	Irritably
Idly	Improbably	Indefinitely	Innately	Internally
Ignominiously	Improperly	Independently	Innocently	Intimately
Ignorantly	Improvidently	Indescribably	Innocently	Intolerable
Ill-advised	Impudently	Indifferently	Inquisitively	Intrepidly
Illegibly	Impurely	Indigently	Instantly	Intricately
Illicitly	In addition	Indignantly	Intensely	Intriguing
Illustriously	In tandem	Indirectly	Innocuously	Intriguingly
Imaginative	Inadequately	Indiscriminately	Inoffensively	Intrinsically
Imaginatively	Inadvertently	Individually	Inopportunely	Invaluably
Immaculately	Inboard	Indolently	Inordinately	Inventively
Immeasurably	Incalculably	Indoor	Insanely	Inversely
Immediately	Incessantly	Indubitably	Insatiably	Invidiously
Immensely	Incidentally	Indulgently	Inscrutably	Invisibly
Immodestly	Incisively	Industriously	Insensitively	Involuntarily
Immutably	Including	Ineffectively	Inshore	Involuntary
Impartially	Inclusively	Ineffectually	Insincerely	Inwards

Impeccably	Incognito	Inefficiently	Insistently	Irately
Imperceptivity	Incoherently	Inevitably	Insofar	Ironically
Imperiously	Incommunicado	Inexorably	Insomuch	Irrationally
Impermanent	Incompetent	Infallibly	Instantaneous	Irrefutably
Impetuously	Incompetently	Infectiously	Intellectually	Irregularly
Implausibly	Inconsiderate	Infinitesimally	Intelligently	Irrelevantly
Implicitly	Inconsiderately	Infirmly	Intensely	Irretrievably
Imploringly	Inconsolable	Informally	Intensified	Irrevocably
Impolitely	Incorrectly	Infrequently	Intensively	Irritably
Importantly	Incorrigibly	Ingenuously	Intentionally	
Imposingly	Incredibly			

— J —

Jaggedly	Jocosely	Jovially	Joyously	Justly
Jealously	Jointly	Joyfully	Jubilantly	Just
Jerkily	Jollily	judiciously	Judgmentally	Just now

— K —

Keenly	Kindheartedly	Knavishly	Knowledgeably	Kookily
Kiddingly	Kindly	Knowingly		

— L —

Laboriously	Laterally	Lengthwise	Listlessly	Loudly
Lackadaisically	Lavishly	Leniently	Literally	Lovingly
Laconically	Lawfully	Less	Little	Lowly
Laggardly	Laxly	Lethargically	Lively	Low
Lamely	Lazily	Lewdly	Loftily	Lower
Landward	Least	Liberally	Logically	Loyally
Languidly	Leastwise	Lightheartedly	Logistically	Lucidly
Largely	Left	Light-heartedly	Lone	Luckily
Last	Left-handed	Lightly	Longingly	Lugubriously
Lastingly	Legally	Like	Loosely	Luridly
Late	Legibly	Likely	Lopsided	Lustily
Lately	Legitimately	Limply	Lordly	Luxuriously
Later	Leisurely	Likewise	Lots	

— M —

Madly	Marvelously	Medically	Militantly	Monthly
Maddeningly	Masochistically	Meekly	Mindfully	Mostly
Magically	Massively	Melodically	Minimally	Moodily
Magisterially	Masterfully	Memorably	Minutely	Morally
Magnanimously	Materially	Menacingly	Miraculously	Morbidly
Magnificently	Maternal	Menially	Mirthfully	More

Mainly	Maternally	Mentally	Mischievously	Moreover
Majestically	Mathematically	Mercifully	Miserably	Morosely
Maladroitly	Maturely	Mercilessly	Misguidedly	Mortally
Malevolently	Mawkishly	Meritoriously	Mistakenly	Mostly
Maliciously	Maybe	Merrily	Mistrustfully	Much
Malignantly	Mayhap	Messily	Mockingly	Mundanely
Manfully	Meagerly	Methodically	Moderately	Munificently
Manically	Meaningfully	Meticulously	Modestly	Musically
Manifestly	Mechanically	Middling	Momentarily	Mutually
Manually	Meanly	Mightily	Monetarily	Mysteriously
Marginally	Meantime	Mildly	Monstrously	Mystically
Markedly	Meanwhile			

— N —

Naively	Nearby	Never	Nonchalantly	Not quite
Nakedly	Nearly	Nevertheless	None	Nothing
Namely	Neatly	Newly	Nonetheless	Noticeably
Nastily	Necessarily	Next	None-the-less	Notoriously
Nationally	Needful	Next to	Nonstop	Notwithstanding
Nattily	Needs	Nicely	Normally	Now
Naturally	Nefarious	Nocturnal	North	Now and then
Naughtily	Nefariously	Nocturnally	Northerly	Nowadays
Nautically	Negatively	Noiselessly	Northward	Nowhere
Nay	Nervously	Noisily	Northwest	Numbly
Near	Newly			

— O —

Obdurately	Offensively	Only	Ordinarily	Outside
Obediently	Officially	On-stream	Organically	Over
Objectively	Ominously	Onward	Originally	Over and over
Obliquely	Officially	Opaquely	Ornately	Overall
Obnoxiously	Officiously	Openly	Ostensibly	Overboard
Obscurely	Offshore	Overtly	Other	Overconfidently
Obsessively	Offstage	Opposite	Otherwise	Overhand
Obstreperously	Oft	Oppositely	Out	Overhead
Obstructively	Often	Oppressively	Out loud	Overland
Obtrusively	Omnivorously	Optically	Outdoors	Overly
Obviously	On high	Optimistically	Out-of-doors	Overmuch
Occasionally	Once	Opulently	Outrageously	Overseas
Oddly	One-one-one	Orally	Outright	Owlishly
Odiously				

— P —

Painfully	Perforce	Placidly	Practicably	Profanely
painlessly	Perfunctorily	Plain	Practically	Professionally
Palpably	Perhaps	Plainly	Pragmatically	Proficiently
Painstakingly	Perilously	Playfully	Prayerfully	Profitably
Paradoxically	Periodically	Pleasantly	Precariously	Profoundly
Part	Permanently	Pleasingly	Preceded	Profusely
Partially	Permissively	Plentifully	Preciously	Prominently
Particularly	Perniciously	Plumb	Precipitously	Promiscuously
Partly	Perpetually	Poetically	Precisely	Promptly
Passably	Personally	Poignantly	Preferably	Pronto
Passionately	Perspicuously	Pointblank	Prematurely	Properly
Passively	Persuasively	Pointedly	Presently	Prophetically
Paternally	Perversely	Politely	Presto	Prosperously
Pathetically	Pessimistically	Politically	Pretentiously	Protectively
Patiently	Pettishly	Polyphonically	Prettily	Proudly
Patriotically	Petulantly	Poorly	Pretty	Providently
Peculiarly	Phlegmatically	Popularly	Previously	Provisionally
Peevishly	Physically	Portentously	Primarily	Provocatively
Pejoratively	Pictorially	Positively	Principally	Pugnaciously
Pell-mell	Piecemeal	Possibly	Prior	Punctually
Penitently	Piggyback	Posthaste	Privately	Pungently
Penuriously	Pit-a-pat	Posthumously	Pro	Punitively
Perceptibly	Piteously	Potentially	Probably	Purely
Perceptively	Pithily	Potently	Prodigiously	Purportedly
Perchance	Pitifully	Powerfully	Productively	Purposely
Perfectly	Pitilessly	Powerlessly		

— Q —

Quaintly	Queasily	Questionably	Quietly	Quickly
Quaintly	Queerly	Questioningly	Quirkily	Quietly
Qualitatively	Querulously	Quicker	Quizzically	Quite

— R —

Racially	Readily	Relatively	Respectfully	Rigidly
Radiantly	Real	Relentlessly	Respectively	Righteously
Radically	Realistically	Reliably	Resplendently	Rigorously
Rakishly	Really	Reluctantly	Responsibly	Robustly
Rancorously	Rearward	Remarkably	Restfully	Romantically

Randomly
Rapacious
Rapaciously
Rapidly
Rapturously

Reasonably
Reassuringly
Recklessly
Recently
Red

Remotely
Repeatedly
Reprehensively
Reproachfully
Repulsively

Restlessly
Reverently
Reversibly
Rhapsodically
Richly

Rosily
Roughly
Round
Roundly
Routinely

Rarely
Rascally
Rather
Rattling
Raucously

Red-handed
Redoubtably
Regardless
Regretfully
Regularly

Reputably
Reputedly
Resentfully
Resolutely
Resoundingly

Ridiculously
Right
Right away
Rightfully
Rightly

Rudely
Ruefully
Ruggedly
Rustically
Ruthlessly

Ravenously

— S —

Sadistically
Sadly
Safely
Scarcely
Scarily

Serendipitous
Serenely
Seriously
Severally
Severely

Singly
Singularly
Sinuously
Sizably
Skeptically

Some
Someday
Somehow
Sometime
Sometimes

Spryly
Spuriously
Square
Squarely
Squarely

Saintly
Salaciously
Sanely
Sarcastically
Sardonically

Sexually
Shabbily
Shakily
Shamefully
Sharply

Skyward
Slam-bang
Slantways
Slantwise
Slapdash

Someway
Somewhat
Somewhere
Soon
Sorely

Squeamishly
Staggering
Staidly
Stark
Startlingly

Satisfyingly
Saucily
Savagely
Scandalously
Scantily

Sheepishly
Shiftily
Shockingly
Shoddily
Short

Slavishly
Sleazily
Sleekly
Sleepily
Slick

Sorrowfully
Sort of
Soundly
Sour
Sourly

Statically
Staunchly
Steadfastly
Steadily
Stiffly

Scarcely
Scientifically
Scornfully
Scot-free
Scrupulously

Shortly
Shortsightedly
Shrewdly
Shrilly
Shyly

Slightly
Sloppily
Slovenly
Slow
Slowly

South
Southeasterly
Southeastward
Southwards
Southwestward

Stilly
Stoutly
Straight
Straightaway
Strenuously

Scurrilously
Searchingly
Securely
Seasonally
Second

Sickly
Sidearm
Sidelong
Sidesaddle
Sideward

Sluggishly
Smack
Smack-dab
Smartly
Smilingly

Spaciously
Sparingly
Sparsely
Spasmodically
Specially

Strictly
Strongly
Sturdily
Submissively
Substantially

Secondarily	Sideways	Smoothly	Specifically	Succinctly
Secretively	Sidewise	Snappily	Speciously	Suitably
Secretly	Sightlessly	Soberly	Spectacularly	Summarily
Sedately	Similarly	Socially	Speedily	Sumptuously
Sedulously	Simplistically	Softheartedly	Spiritedly	Super
Seemingly	Simply	Softly	Spiritlessly	Supposedly
Seldom	Simultaneously	Soldierly	Spiritually	Surely
Self-consciously	Since	Sole	Spitefully	Suspiciously
Selfishly	Sincerely	Solely	Splashily	Swift
Self-righteously	Sinfully	Solemnly	Splendidly	Swiftly
Sensibly	Single	Solidly	Sporadically	Swimmingly
Sensually	Singlehanded	Solo	Spotlessly	Sympathetically
Sequentially	Singlehandedly	Somberly	Sprightly	

— T —

Tactical	Tightly	Therewith	Tirelessly	Trailing
Tardily	Theatrically	Thickly	Tiresomely	Transcendentally
Tartly	Then	Thinly	To boot	Transparently
Tastefully	Thence	Third	To the rear of	Transversely
Tearfully	Thenceforth	Thoroughly	Today	Treacherous
Technically	There	Thoroughly	Together	Tremendously
Tediously	Thereabouts	Thoughtfully	Tolerably	Trenchantly
Tellingly	Thereafter	Through	Tolerably	Trippingly
Tenaciously	Thereby	Throughout	Tomorrow	Triumphantly
Tendentiously	Therefore	Thus	Tonally	Truly
Tenderly	Therein	Thus far	Too	Trustfully
Tensely	Thereof	Time and again	Topside	Tryingly
Terribly	Thereon	Tingly	Topsy-turvy	Tunelessly
Tersely	Thereto	Tiredly	Totally	Typically
Terribly	Thereupon	Tiredly	Tragically	Tyrannically
Thankfully				

— U —

Ultimately	Underneath	Uniformly	Unsatisfactorily	Upstairs
Uniformly	Undersea	Unimpressively	Unsparingly	Upstate
Unabashedly	Undersell	Unnaturally	Unspeakably	Upstream
Unaccountably	Understandable	Unnecessarily	Unsuitable	Upward
Unacceptably	Understandably	Unique	Until	Upwardly
Unaided	Understandingly	Unlawfully	Untimely	Upwind
Unaware	Undoubtedly	Unlike	Unusual	Urgently
Unbearably	Unduly	Unmercifully	Unwittingly	Usefully
Unblushingly	Uneasily	Unmistakably	Up	Uselessly
Uncharitably	Unethically	Unnecessarily	Upfront	Usually

Uncomfortably	Unexpectedly	Unpredictably	Upgrade	Utterly
Unconscionably	Unevenly	Unpretentiously	Uphill	Upwardly
Undeniably	Unfailingly	Unquestionably	Upon	Urgently
Under	Unfeelingly	Unreasonably	Uppermost	Usefully
Underhandedly	Unfortunately	Unremittingly	Upriver	Uselessly
Underling	Unhappily	Unreservedly		

— V —

Vacantly	Vast	Verily	Viciously	Visibly
Vaguely	Vehemently	Veritably	Voluntarily	Vitally
Vainly	Vengefully	Versus	Vigorously	Vivaciously
Valiantly	Very	Vertically	Vindictively	Vividly
Vastly	Viciously	Very	Violently	Vocally
Vacuously	Victoriously	Vibrantly	Virtually	Voluminously
Validly	Verbally	Vicariously	Virtuously	Voluntarily
Variously	Verbatim	Vice versa	Virulently	Vulgarly

— W —

Warily	Whacking	Wholesale	Willingly	Worriedly
Warmly	When	Wholly	Willy-nilly	Wrongly
Weakly	Whence	Why	Windward	Woodenly
Wearily	Whenever	Wickedly	Wishfully	Word for word
Well	Where	Widely	Wistfully	Worthily
Wastefully	Whereabouts	Wild	Withal	Wretchedly
Waywardly	Wherefore	Wildly	Within	Wrong
Wearisomely	Whereof	Wildly	Without	Wrongfully
Weekly	Whereupon	Willfully	Wittily	Wrong-headedly
Well	Whimsically	Wisely	Wittingly	Wrongly
Well-nigh	Whither	Wherever	Woefully	Wryly
Westerly	Whole-hog	Willfully	Wonderfully	

— X —

nil

— Y —

Yea	Yearly	Yet	Yonder	Youthfully
Yes	Yesteryear	Yon	Yore	

—Z—

Zealously	zigzag

APPENDIX D
VERB GARDEN

— A —

Abandon	Acquaint	Aim	Apologize	Assert
Abase	Acquiesce	Air	Appall	Assess
Abash	Acquire	Airbrush	Appeal	Assign
Abate	Acquit	Airmail	Appear	Assimilate
Abbreviate	Act	Alarm	Appease	Assist
Abdicate	Activate	Alert	Append	Associate
Abduct	Actualize	Alienate	Appertain	Assort
Abet	Actuate	Alight	Applaud	Assuage
Abhor	Ad lib	Align	Applied	Assume
Abide	Addict	Allay	Apply	Assure
Abnegate	Addle	Allege	Appoint	Astonish
Abolish	Address	Alleviate	Apportion	Astound
Abominate	Adhere	Allocate	Appose	Atomize
Abort	Adjoin	Allot	Appraise	Atone
Abound	Adjourn	Allow	Appreciate	Atrophy
Abrade	Adjudicate	Allude	Apprehend	Attach
Abridge	Adjust	Allure	Apprise	Attack
Abrogate	Ad-lib	Ally	Approach	Attain
Abscond	Administer	Alter	Appropriate	Attempt
Absolve	Admire	Alternate	Approve	Attend
Absorb	Admit	Amalgamate	Approximate	Attest
Abstain	Admonish	Amass	Arbitrate	Attract
Abuse	Adopt	Amaze	Argue	Attribute
Abut	Adore	Amble	Arise	Attune
Accede	Adorn	Ambush	Arm	Auction
Accelerate	Adulate	Ameliorate	Armor	Audit
Accent	Adulterate	Amend	Arouse	Audition
Accentuate	Advance	Amplify	Arraign	Augment
Accept	Advertise	Amputate	Arrange	Augur
Access	Advise	Amuse	Arrest	Authenticate
Acclaim	Advocate	Analyze	Arrive	Author
Acclimate	Aerate	Anchor	Arrogate	Authorize
Accommodate	Affect	Anesthetize	Articulate	Autograph
Accompany	Affiliate	Anger	Ascend	Automate
Accomplish	Affirm	Animate	Ascertain	Avail

Accost
Account
Accredit
Accrue
Accumulate

Accuse
Accustom
Ace
Ache
Achieve

Acknowledge

Affix
Afflict
Affront
Aggrandize
Aggravate

Aggregate
Aggrieve
Agitate
Agonize
Agree

Aid

Annex
Annihilate
Annotate
Announce
Annoy

Annul
Answer
Antagonize
Antedate
Anticipate

Antiquate

Ascribe
Ask
Asphyxiate
Aspire
Assail

Assassinate
Assault
Assay
Assemble
Assent

Avenge
Average
Avert
Avoid
Avouch

Avow
Await
Awaken
Award
Axe

— B —

Back
Backbite
Backfire
Backlash
Backpedal

Backslide
Backtrack
Badger
Bad-mouth
Baffle

Bag
Bail
Bait
Bake
Balance

Balk
Balloon
Bamboozle
Ban
Bandage

Bandy
Bang
Banish
Bank
Bankable

Battle
Bawl
Bayonet
Beam
Bear

Beat
Beautify
Becalm
Beckon
Becloud

Become
Bedazzle
Bedeck
Bedevil
Bedim

Bedraggle
Befall
Befit
Befog
Befoul

Befriend
Befuddle
Beg
Beget
Begin

Besmirch
Bestir
Bestow
Bet
Betray

Betroth
Better
Bewail
Beware
Bewilder

Bewitch
Bicker
Bid
Bide
Bilk

Bill
Billow
Bind
Bite
Blabber

Blackball
Blacklist
Blackmail
Blame
Blanket

Benumb
Bequeath
Berate
Bereave
Beseech

Beset
Besiege
Besmear
Blot
Bloviate

Blow
Bludgeon
Blue-pencil
Bluff
Blunder

Blur
Blurt
Blush
Bluster
Board

Boast
Bobble
Bode
Bog
Boggle

Bore
Borrow
Boss
Botch
Bother

Bottle
Bounce
Bound
Bow
Bowl

Box
Boycott
Brace
Bracket
Brag

Brain
Brainstorm
Brainwash
Brake
Branch

Breach
Break
Breathe
Breed
Brighten

Bankroll	Begrudge	Blaspheme	Boil	Bring
Bankrupt	Beguile	Blast	Bold	Broadcast
Banter	Behave	Blaze	Bolster	Bruise
Bar	Behold	Bleach	Bolt	Brush
Barbecue	Behoove	Bleed	Bomb	Bubbly
Bare	Bejewel	Blemish	Bombard	Budge
Bargain	Belabor	Blend	Bond	Budget
Barge	Belie	Bless	Booby-trap	Buffet
Barnstorm	Believe	Blind	Book	Build
Barrage	Belittle	Blindfold	Boom	Bulldoze
Barricade	Bellow	Blindside	Boomerang	Bump
Barter	Bellyache	Blink	Boost	Burden
Base	Belong	Blister	Boot	Burn
Bash	Belt	Blitz	Bootleg	Bury
Bask	Bemoan	Bloat	Bootlick	Bust
Baste	Bemuse	Block	Booze	Butcher
Bat	Bench	Blockade	Bop	Buy
Bathe	Bend	Blog	Border	Buzz
Batter	Benefit	Bloom		

— C —

Cache	Chat	Comb	Confront	Corrupt
Cackle	Cheat	Combat	Confuse	Cost
Cage	Check	Combine	Congeal	Cough
Cajole	Check-mate	Come	Congratulate	Counsel
Calculate	Cheer	Comfort	Congregate	Count
Calibrate	Cherish	Command	Conk	Counteract
Call	Chew	Commandeer	Connect	Couple
Calm	Chide	Commemorate	Connote	Court
Camouflage	Chill	Commence	Conquer	Cover
Camp	Chisel	Commend	Consent	Covet
Campaign	Choke	Comment	Conserve	Cower
Can	Choose	Commiserate	Consider	Crack
Cancel	Chop	Commission	Consign	Careen
Canonize	Choreograph	Commit	Consist	Caress
Canvass	Chuck	Communicate	Corral	Caricature
Capitalize	Cinch	Compact	Correct	Carouse
Capitulate	Circle	Confiscate	Correlate	Carp
Captivate	Circulate	Conflict	Correspond	Carry
Capture	Colonize	Conform	Corroborate	Carve
Care	Color	Confound	Corrode	Cast

Castigate	Clasp	Complain	Constitute	Crash
Catalog	Classify	Complement	Constrain	Crave
Catch	Clean	Complete	Constrict	Crawl
Categorize	Clear	Complicate	Construct	Crease
Cater	Cleave	Compliment	Construe	Create
Caterwaul	Clench	Comply	Consult	Credit
Caution	Click	Compose	Consume	Creep
Cause	Climb	Comprehend	Contact	Crimp
Cavort	Cling	Compress	Contain	Cringe
Cease	Clip	Comprise	Contaminate	Criticize
Celebrate	Cloak	Compromise	Contemplate	Critique
Cement	Clog	Conceal	Contend	Croak
Censure	Close	Concede	Contest	Croon
Certify	Clot	Conceive	Continue	Cross
Challenge	Clothe	Concentrate	Contort	Cross-examine
Champion	Club	Conceptualize	Contract	Crouch
Chance	Clutter	Concern	Contradict	Crowd
Change	Coach	Conciliate	Contribute	Cruise
Char	Coax	Conclude	Contrive	Crusade
Characterize	Coddle	Concoct	Control	Crush
Charge	Coerce	Concur	Convene	Cry
Charm	Cohabit	Condemn	Converse	Cue
Chart	Cohere	Condense	Convert	Cuff
Charter	Coil	Condescend	Convey	Cull
Chase	Coin	Condone	Convict	Culminate
Chasten	Collaborate	Conduct	Convince	Cultivate
Chastise	Collapse	Confer	Cook	Curb
Circumscribe	Collect	Confess	Cool	Cure
Circumvent	Collide	Confide	Cooperate	Curl
Cite	Compare	Confine	Coordinate	Curse
Civilize	Compel	Confirm	Copy	Curtail
Claim	Compensate	Console	Copyright	Curve
Clap	Compete	Consolidate	Corner	Customize
Clarify	Compile	Conspire	Cramp	Cycle

— D —

Dabble	Dehydrate	Detain	Discredit	Divine
Dam	Delay	Detect	Discriminate	Divorce
Damage	Delegate	Deter	Discuss	Divulge
Dampen	Delete	Deteriorate	Disembark	Do
Dance	Deliberate	Determine	Disengage	Doctor

Dangle	Delight	Detest	Disfavor	Document
Dare	Delineate	Detonate	Disfigure	Dodge
Dart	Deliver	Detour	Disgorge	Does
Dash	Delude	Devalue	Disgrace	Domesticate
Date	Demand	Devastate	Disguise	Dominate
Daub	Demean	Develop	Disgust	Domineer
Dawdle	Demolish	Deviate	Dishonor	Donate
Daze	Demonize	Devise	Disillusion	Doodle
Dazzle	Demonstrate	Devitalize	Disinfect	Doom
Deactivate	Demoralize	Devote	Disintegrate	Double
Deal	Demote	Devour	Dislike	Double-cross
Debase	Demur	Diagnose	Dislodge	Doubt
Debate	Demystify	Dicker	Dismantle	Douse
Debauch	Denigrate	Dictate	Dismay	Down
Debilitate	Denote	Die	Dismember	Downgrade
Debunk	Denounce	Diet	Dismiss	Downplay
Debut	Dent	Differ	Dismount	Downscale
Decay	Denunciate	Differentiate	Disown	Doze
Deceive	Deny	Diffuse	Disparage	Draft
Decide	Deodorize	Dig	Dispatch	Drag
Decimate	Depart	Digest	Dispense	Drain
Decipher	Depend	Digitize	Disperse	Dramatize
Declare	Depict	Dignify	Display	Draw
Decline	Deplete	Digress	Displease	Dread
Decode	Deplore	Dilate	Dispose	Dream
Decorate	Deport	Dim	Disprove	Drench
Decoy	Deposit	Diminish	Dispute	Dress
Decrease	Deprecate	Dine	Disqualify	Drift
Decry	Depress	Ding	Disrobe	Drill
Dedicate	Deprive	Direct	Dissect	Drink
Deduce	Derail	Disable	Disseminate	Drip
Deem	Derange	Disagree	Dissent	Drive
Deepen	Deride	Disallow	Dissipate	Drop
Deface	Derive	Disappear	Dissolve	Drown
Defame	Descend	Disappoint	Distance	Drub
Default	Describe	Disapprove	Distill	Drum
Defeat	Desecrate	Disarm	Distinguish	Dry
Defend	Desensitize	Disavow	Distort	Duck
Defer	Desert	Disband	Distract	Dumbfound
Defile	Deserve	Disburse	Distress	Dump

Define	Design	Discard	Distribute	Dunk
Deflate	Designate	Discharge	Distrust	Dupe
Deflect	Desire	Discipline	Disturb	Duplicate
Defoliate	Desist	Disclaim	Ditch	Dust
Deform	Despair	Disclose	Dive	Dwarf
Defraud	Despise	Discolor	Diverge	Dwell
Defray	Destroy	Discombobulate	Divert	Dwindle
Defy	Detach	Discourage	Divest	Dye
Degenerate	Detail	Discover	Divide	Dynamite
Degrade				

— E —

Early	Emblazon	Enliven	Espouse	Excoriate
Earmark	Embody	Enmesh	Espy	Exculpate
Earn	Embolden	Ennoble	Essay	Excuse
Ease	Embrace	Enquire	Establish	Execute
Eat	Embroider	Enrage	Esteem	Exemplify
Eavesdrop	Embroil	Enrapture	Estimate	Exempt
Ebb	Emcee	Enrich	Evaluate	Exercise
Eccentric	Emend	Enroll	Examine	Exert
Echo	Emerge	Ensconce	Exceed	Exhale
Eclipse	Emigrate	Enshrine	Excite	Exhaust
Economize	Eminent	Enshroud	Excuse	Exhaustive
Edge	Emit	Enslave	Execute	Exhibit
Edify	Empathize	Ensnare	Exercise	Exhilarate
Edit	Employ	Ensue	Exhibit	Exhort
Educate	Empower	Ensure	Exist	Exile
Educe	Empty	Entail	Expand	Exist
Efface	Emulate	Entangle	Expect	Exonerate
Effect	Enable	Enter	Expedite	Expand
Effectuate	Enact	Entertain	Experiment	Expatiate
Effuse	Enamor	Enthrall	Explain	Expect
Egg	Encapsulate	Enthuse	Explode	Expedite
Eject	Encase	Entice	Express	Expel
Elaborate	Enchant	Entitle	Extend	Expend
Elapse	Encircle	Entomb	Extract	Experience
Elate	Enclose	Entrance	Estrange	Experiment
Elbow	Encompass	Entrap	Etch	Expiate
Elect	Encounter	Entreat	Eulogize	Expire
Electrify	Encourage	Entrench	Euthanize	Explain
Electrocute	Encroach	Entrust	Evacuate	Explode
Elegant	Encumber	Enumerate	Evade	Exploit

Elevate	Endanger	Enunciate	Evaluate	Explore
Elicit	Endear	Envelop	Evangelize	Expose
Eliminate	Endeavor	Envenom	Evaporate	Expound
Elongate	Endorse	Envisage	Evict	Express
Eloquent	Endow	Envision	Eviscerate	Expropriate
Elucidate	Endure	Envy	Evoke	Expunge
Elude	Energize	Epitomize	Exacerbate	Extemporize
Emaciate	Enervate	Equalize	Exact	Extend
e-mail	Enfeeble	Equate	Exaggerate	Exterminate
Emanate	Enforce	Equip	Exalt	Externalize
Emancipate	Engage	Equivocate	Examine	Extinguish
Emasculate	Engineer	Eradicate	Exasperate	Extol
Embalm	Engrave	Erase	Excavate	Extort
Embargo	Engulf	Erect	Exceed	Extract
Embark	Enhance	Erode	Excel	Extradite
Embarrass	Enjoin	Err	Except	Extricate
Embed	Enjoy	Erupt	Exchange	Exude
Embellish	Enlarge	Escalate	Excite	Exult
Embezzle	Enlighten	Escape	Exclaim	Eye
Embitter	Enlist	Escort	Exclude	Eyeball

— F —

Fabricate	Fend	Flank	Foil	Found
Face	Ferment	Flap	Foist	Fracture
Facilitate	Ferret	Flare	Fold	Fragment
Fade	Fertilize	Flash	Follow	Frame
Fail	Fester	Flatten	Foment	Fraternize
Faint	Festoon	Flatter	Fondle	Frazzle
Fake	Fetch	Flaunt	Fool	Freak-out
Fall	Fib	Flavor	Forage	Free
Falsify	Fiddle	Flee	Forbear	Freelance
Falter	Fidget	Fleece	Forbid	Free-wheel
Familiarize	Field	Flex	Force	Freeze
Famish	Fight	Flick	Forebode	Freeze-dry
Fan	Figure	Flinch	Forecast	Frequent
Fancy	Filch	Fling	Foreclose	Freshen
Fantasize	File	Flip	Foredoom	Fret
Fare	Filibuster	Flirt	Forego	Frighten
Farm	Fill	Flit	Foreordain	Frisk
Fascinate	Fillet	Float	Foresee	Fritter
Fashion	Film	Flock	Foreshadow	Frizzle
Fast	Filter	Flog	Foreshorten	Frolic

Fasten	Finagle	Flood	Forestall	Frost
Father	Finance	Floor	Foreswear	Frown
Fathom	Find	Flop	Foretell	Frustrate
Fatigue	Fine	Flounder	Forewarn	Fry
Fault	Finesse	Flourish	Forfeit	Fudge
Favor	Fine-tune	Flout	Forge	Fulfill
Fawn	Finger	Flow	Forget	Fulminate
Fax	Finish	Flower	Forgive	Fumble
Faze	Fire	Flub	Forgo	Fume
Fear	Fireproof	Fluctuate	Form	Function
Feast	Fish	Fluff	Formalize	Fund
Featherbed	Fit	Flummox	Formulate	Funnel
Feature	Fix	Flunk	Forsake	Furnish
Feed	Fizzle	Flurry	Forswear	Furrow
Feel	Flabbergast	Fluster	Fortify	Further
Feign	Flagellate	Flutter	Forward	Fuse
Fell	Flail	Fly	Foster	Fuss
Fence	Flame	Focus	Foul	

— G —

Gab	Ghostwrite	Goldbrick	Grin	Gush
Gaff	Giggle	Golf	Grind	Gut
Gag	Gild	Goof	Grip	Guttural
Gain	Gird	Google	Gripe	Guzzle
Gainsay	Girdle	Gore	Groan	Gyp
Gallivant	Give	Gorge	Groom	Gyrate
Gallop	Glaciate	Gormandize	Groove	Gather
Galvanize	Gladden	Gossip	Grope	Gaze
Gamble	Glamorize	Gouge	Grouch	Generate
Gander	Glance	Govern	Ground	Get
Gape	Glare	Grab	Group	Give
Garble	Glaze	Grace	Grouse	Glow
Garden	Glean	Grade	Grovel	Glue
Gargle	Glide	Graduate	Grow	Govern
Garner	Glimpse	Grandstand	Growl	Grab
Garnish	Glint	Grant	Grub	Graduate
Garrote	Glisten	Graph	Grudge	Grate
Gash	Glitter	Grapple	Grumble	Grease
Gasp	Gloat	Grasp	Grunt	Greet
Gather	Glorify	Grate	Guarantee	Grin

Gauge	Gloss	Gratify	Guard	Grind
Gawk	Glow	Graven	Guess	Grip
Gaze	Glower	Gravitate	Guffaw	Groan
Generalize	Glue	Graze	Guide	Grow
Generate	Gnarl	Grease	Guild	Guarantee
Genuflect	Gnash	Green	Guillotine	Guard
Germinate	Gnaw	Greet	Gull	Guess
Gerrymander	Goad	Grieve	Gulp	Guide
Gesticulate	Gobble	Grill	Gun	Gladden
Gesture	Goggle	Grimace	Gurgle	Gratify

— H —

Habituate	Harness	Hem	Hock	Howl
Hack	Harpoon	Hemorrhage	Hoe	Huddle
Haggle	Harvest	Henpeck	Hogtie	Hug
Hail	Hassle	Herald	Hoist	Hula
Hallow	Hasten	Herd	Hold	Hum
Hallucinate	Hatch	Hesitate	Holler	Humanize
Halt	Hate	Hew	Hollow	Humble
Hammer	Haul	Hex	Homogenize	Humiliate
Hamper	Haunt	Hibernate	Hone	Humor
Hamstring	Have	Hide	Honk	Hunger
Hand	Hawk	High-five	Honor	Hunt
Handcuff	Hazard	Highlight	Hoodwink	Hurdle
Handicap	Head	Hightail	Hook	Hurl
Handle	Heal	Hijack	Hoot	Hurry
Handpick	Heap	Hike	Hop	Hurt
Hang	Hear	Hinder	Hope	Hurtle
Hanker	Hearten	Hinge	Horde	Husband
Happen	Heat	Hint	Horrify	Hush
Harangue	Heave	Hire	Horsewhip	Hustle
Harass	Heckle	Hiss	Hose	Hydrate
Harbor	Hedge	Hit	Hotfoot	Hype
Harden	Heed	Hitch	Hound	Hyperextend
Hark	Heel	Hitchhike	House	Hyperventilate
Harkin	Heighten	Hoard	Housebreak	Hypnotize
Harm	Heist	Hoax	Hover	Hypothesize
Harmonize	Help	Hobnob		

— I —

Idealize	Import	Induce	Inspect	Interrupt
Identify	Impose	Induct	Inspire	Intersect
Idle	Impound	Indulge	Install	Intersperse
Idolize	Impoverish	Inebriate	Instigate	Intertwine
Ignite	Impress	Infatuate	Instill	Intervene
Ignore	Imprint	Infect	Institute	Interview
Ill-treat	Imprison	Infer	Institutionalize	Interweave
Illuminate	Improve	Infest	Instruct	Intimate
Illustrate	Improvise	Infiltrate	Insulate	Intimidate
Imagine	Impugn	Inflame	Insult	Intoxicate
Imbed	Impute	Inflate	Insure	Intrigue
Imbibe	Inactivate	Inflict	Integrate	Introduce
Imitate	Inanimate	Influence	Intend	Intrude
Immerse	Inaugurate	Inform	Intensify	Inundate
Immigrate	Incapacitate	Infringe	Inter	Inure
Immobilize	Incarcerate	Infuriate	Interact	Invade
Immolate	Incense	Infuse	intercede	Invalidate
Immortalize	Incinerate	Ingest	Intercept	Inveigle
Immunize	Incite	Ingrain	Interchange	Invent
Impact	Incline	Ingratiate	Interconnect	Inventory
Impair	Include	Inhabit	Interest	Invert
Impale	Inconvenience	Inhale	Interface	Invest
Impart	Incorporate	Inherit	Interfere	Investigate
Impassion	Increase	Inhibit	Interject	Invigorate
Impeach	Incriminate	Initiate	Interlace	Invite
Impede	Incubate	Inject	Interlock	Involve
Impel	Inculcate	Injure	Interlope	Irk
Imperil	Incur	Inlay	Intermingle	Irradiate
Impersonate	Indemnify	Innovate	Intermix	Irrigate
Impinge	Indentify	Inoculate	Intern	Irritate
Implant	Index	Input	Internalize	Isolate
Implement	Indicate	Inquire	Interpolate	Issue
Implicate	Indict	Inscribe	Interpose	Itch
Implode	Individualize	Insert	Interpret	Itemize
Implore	Indoctrinate	Insinuate	Interrogate	Iterate
Imply	Indorse	Insist		

—J—

Jab	Jar	Jet	Jog	Joust
Jabber	Jaundiced	Jettison	Join	Judge
Jack	Jaunt	Jiggle	Joke	Juggle
Jackknife	Jawbone	Jilt	Jolt	Jumble
Jade	Jeer	Jimmy	Josh	Jump
Jail	Jell	Jinx	Jostle	Junk
Jam	Jeopardize	Jitterbug	Jot	Justify
Jam-pack	Jerk	Jockey	Journey	Juxtapose
Jangle	Jest			

—K—

Kayo	Kibosh	Kidnap	Knead	Knock
Keelhaul	Kick	Kill	Kneel	Knot
Keep	Kick-start	Kindle	Knife	Know
Keyboard	Kid	Kiss	Knit	Kowtow

—L—

Label	Laugh	Let	Liquefy	Look
Labor	Launch	Level	Liquidate	Loom
Lacerate	Launder	Leverage	List	Loop
Lack	Lavish	Levitate	Listen	Loosen
Ladle	Lay	Levy	Litigate	Loot
Lag	Leach	Libel	Litter	Lop
Lambaste	Lead	Liberalize	Live	Lose
Lament	Leak	Liberate	Load	Lounge
Lampoon	Lean	License	Loaf	Love
Lance	Leap	Lick	Loan	Lower
Land	Learn	Lie	Loathe	Lubricate
Landscape	Lease	Lift	Lob	Lug
Languish	Leash	Light	Lobby	Lull
Lap	Leave	Lighten	Localize	Lumber
Lapse	Lecture	Like	Locate	Lump
Larrup	Leech	Liken	Lock	Lunge
Lash	Legalize	Limit	Lodge	Lurch
Lasso	Legislate	Limp	Log	Lure
Last	Legitimize	Line	Loiter	Lurk
Latch	Lend	Linger	Loll	Lust
Lateral	Lengthen	Link	Lollygag	Luxuriate
Laud	Lessen	Lionize	Long	Lynch

—M—

Machinate	Mass	Migrate	Misspell	Mortify
Machine	Massacre	Mildew	Mistake	Mosey
Madden	Massage	Militarize	Mistreat	Mothball
Magnetize	Master	Militate	Mistrust	Motion
Magnify	Mastermind	Milk	Misunderstand	Motivate
Mail	Match	Mimic	Misuse	Motor
Maim	Mate	Mince	Mitigate	Mould
Maintain	Materialize	Mind	Mix	Mount
Make	Matter	Mine	Moan	Mourn
Malfunction	Mature	Mingle	Mob	Move
Malign	Maul	Minimize	Mobilize	Mow
Malinger	Maximize	Minister	Mock	Muckrake
Maltreat	Mean	Mint	Model	Muddle
Man	Meander	Mirror	Moderate	Muddy
Manage	Measure	Misapprehend	Modernize	Muff
Maneuver	Meddle	Misappropriate	Modify	Muffle
Mangle	Mediate	Misbehave	Modulate	Mug
Manhandle	Medicate	Miscalculate	Moisten	Mull
Manifest	Meditate	Miscarry	Mold	Multiply
Manipulate	Meet	Misconstrue	Molest	Mumble
Manufacture	Mellow	Misfire	Mollify	Mummify
Map	Melt	Misinform	Mollycoddle	Munch
March	Memorialize	Misjudge	Monitor	Murder
Marginalize	Memorize	Mislay	Monopolize	Murmur
Marinate	Menace	Mislead	Mooch	Mushroom
Mark	Mend	Mismanage	Moonlight	Muster
Market	Mention	Misplace	Moor	Mutate
Maroon	Mentor	Misplay	Moot	Mute
Marry	Merge	Misprice	Mop	Mutilate
Marshal	Merit	Misquote	Mope	Mutiny
Marvel	Mesh	Misread	Moralize	Mutter
Mash	Mesmerize	Misrepresent	Morph	Muzzle
Mask	Microwave	Miss	Mortgage	Mystify
Masquerade	Miff			

—N—

Nab	Navigate	Nest	Nod	Notify
Nag	Near	Nestle	Nominate	Nourish
Nail	Neaten	Neutralize	Nonplus	Nudge
Name	Necessitate	Nibble	Normalize	Nuke
Nap	Need	Nick	Nose-dive	Nullify

Narrate	Needle	Niggle	Nosh	Number
Narrow	Negate	Nip	Notch	Nurse
Nationalize	Neglect	Nitpick	Note	Nurture
Naturalize	Negotiate	Nix	Notice	Nuzzle
Nauseate				

—O—

Obey	Opine	Outgo	Overcharge	Override
Obfuscate	Oppose	Outgrow	Overcome	Overrule
Object	Oppress	Outguess	Overdo	Overrun
Obligate	Opt	Outlast	Overdose	Oversee
Oblige	Orate	Outlaw	Overdraw	Overshadow
Obliterate	Orbit	Outline	Overdress	Overshoot
Obscure	Orchestrate	Outlive	Overestimate	Oversimplify
Observe	Ordain	Outmaneuver	Overflow	Oversleep
Obsess	Order	Outmatch	Overgrow	Overstate
Obstruct	Organize	Outplay	Overhang	Overstay
Obtain	Orient	Outrage	Overhaul	Overstep
Obtrude	Orient	Outrank	Overhear	Overstuff
Obviate	Originate	Outrun	Overheat	Overtake
Occupy	Orientate	Outshine	Overindulge	Overtax
Occur	Oscillate	Outsmart	Overlap	Overthrow
Offend	Ossify	Outsource	Overlay	Overturn
Offer	Ostracize	Outstretch	Overlie	Overwhelm
Officiate	Oust	Outstrip	Overload	Overwork
Offload	Outbid	Outvote	Overlook	Owe
Offset	Outclass	Outwear	Overmatch	Own
Ogle	Outdo	Outweigh	Overpower	Oxidize
Omit	Outfit	Outwit	Overprice	Oxygenate
Ooze	Outflank	Overachieve	Overprotect	Overreach
Open	Outfox	Overact	Overrate	Overreact
Operate				

—P—

Pace	Perceive	Play	Predispose	Prolong
Pacify	Perch	Plead	Predominate	Promenade
Pack	Percolate	Please	Preempt	Promise
Package	Perfect	Pledge	Preen	Promote
Pad	Perform	Plop	Prefabricate	Prompt
Paddle	Perfume	Plot	Prefer	Promulgate
Page	Perish	Plow	Prejudge	Pronounce
Paid	Perjure	Pluck	Prejudice	Prop
Paint	Permeate	Plug	Premeditate	Propagate
Palpitate	Permit	Plumb	Preoccupy	Propel

Pamper	Perpetuate	Plummet	Preordain	Prophesy
Pan	Perplex	Plunder	prepackage	Propose
Pander	Persecute	Plunge	Prepare	Proposition
Panhandle	Persevere	Ply	Prepay	Prorate
Panic	Persist	Poach	Prerecord	Proscribe
Pant	Personalize	Pocket	Presage	Prosecute
Parachute	Perspire	Point	Prescribe	Proselytize
Parade	Persuade	Poison	Present	Prospect
Paralyze	Pertain	Poke	Preserve	Prosper
Paraphrase	Perturb	Police	Preset	Protect
Pardon	Peruse	Polish	Preside	Protest
Pare	Pervade	Politicize	Press	Protrude
Park	Pervert	Poll	Pressure	Prove
Parlay	Pester	Pollute	Prestidigitate	Provide
Parody	Pet	Pommel	Presume	Provoke
Parole	Petition	Ponder	Presuppose	Prowl
Parrot	Petrify	Pontificate	Pretend	Prune
Parse	Philosophize	Pooh-pooh	Prevail	Pry
Part	Phone	Pool	Prevaricate	Publicize
Partake	Photoengrave	Pop	Prevent	Publish
Participate	Photograph	Populate	Preview	Pucker
Party	Pick	Portend	Prey	Puff
Pass	Picket	Portray	Prick	Pull
Paste	Pickle	Pose	Prime	Pulsate
Pat	Picture	Position	Primitive	Pulverize
Patch	Piddle	Possess	Primp	Pummel
Patent	Pierce	Post	Print	Pump
Patrol	Pile	Postpone	Prioritize	Punch
Patronize	Pilfer	Postulate	Prize	Punctuate
Pattern	Pillage	Pounce	Probe	Puncture
Pauperize	Pillory	Pound	Proceed	Punish
Pause	Pilot	Pour	Process	Punt
Pave	Pin	Pour	Proclaim	Purchase
Paw	Pinch	Pout	Procrastinate	Puree
Pawn	Pine	Powder	Procure	Purge
Pay	Pinpoint	Power	Prod	Purify
Peck	Pioneer	Practice	Produce	Purloin
Pedal	Pique	Praise	Profane	Purport
Peddle	Pirate	Prance	Profess	Purr
Peek	Pirouette	Prattle	Proffer	Pursue

Peel	Pitch	Pray	Profile	Purvey
Peep	Pity	Preach	Profit	Push
Peer	Pivot	Prearrange	Profligate	Pussyfoot
Peeve	Placate	Precede	Prognosticate	Put
Pelt	Place	Precipitate	Program	Putrefy
Pen	Plagiarize	Preclude	Progress	Putt
Penalize	Plague	Predestine	Prohibit	Putter
Penetrate	Plan	Predetermine	Project	Puzzle
Pepper	Plant	Predicate	Proliferate	Pyramid
Perambulate	Plaster	Predict		

—Q—

Quack	Qualify	Quaver	Queue	Quip
Quadruple	Quantify	Quell	Quibble	Quit
Quaff	Quarantine	Quench	Quicken	Quiver
Quail	Quarrel	Query	Quick-freeze	Quiz
Quake	Quash	Question	Quiet	Quote

—R—

Radiate	Recount	Relegate	Research	Reward
Rain	Recoup	Relent	Resemble	Rewrite
Raise	Recover	Relieve	Resend	Rhyme
Rank	Recruit	Relinquish	Resent	Ricochet
Ransom	Rectify	Relish	Reserve	Rid
Rant	Recuperate	Relocate	Reset	Ride
Rasp	Recycle	Rely	Reside	Ridicule
Rate	Redecorate	Rely	Resign	Rig
Ratify	Redeem	Remain	Resist	Right
Ration	Redo	Remake	Resolve	Rile
Rationalize	Reduce	Remark	Respect	Ring
Rattle	Reek	Remedy	Respond	Rinse
Ravage	Reel	Remember	Rest	Riot
Rave	Refashion	Remind	Restore	Rip
Ravish	Refer	Remit	Restrain	Ripen
Razz	Refine	Remodel	Restrict	Ripple
Reach	Refinish	Remove	Restructure	Rise
React	Reflect	Remunerate	Result	Risk
Read	Reform	Render	Resume	Rival
Realign	Refrain	Renew	Resuscitate	Rivet
Realize	Refresh	Renounce	Retail	Roam
Ream	Refrigerate	Renovate	Retain	Roar
Reap	Refund	Rent	Retaliate	Roast
Rear	Refurbish	Reorganize	Retard	Rob
Reason	Refuse	Repaid	Retell	Robotize

Reassure	Refute	Repair	Retire	Rock
Reawaken	Regale	Repay	Retrace	Roll
Rebel	Regard	Repeal	Retract	Romance
Rebound	Regenerate	Repeat	Retreat	Romanticize
Rebuff	Register	Repel	Retrieve	Root
Rebuke	Regress	Repent	Return	Rot
Rebut	Regret	Rephrase	Reunite	Rotate
Recall	Regulate	Replace	Revamp	Round
Recapitulate	Regulate	Replenish	Reveal	Rouse
Recapture	Regurgitate	Reply	Revel	Rout
Recede	Rehabilitate	Report	Revenge	Rove
Receive	Rehash	Repossess	Reverberate	Rub
Reciprocate	Rehearse	Represent	Revere	Rubber-stamp
Recite	Reign	Repress	Reverse	Ruffle
Reckon	Reimburse	Reprimand	Revert	Ruin
Recline	Reinforce	Reproach	Review	Rule
Recognize	Reintegrate	Reproduce	Revile	Rumble
Recoil	Reject	Repudiate	Revise	Ruminate
Recollect	Rejoice	Repulse	Revitalize	Rummage
Recommend	Rejuvenate	Request	Revive	Run
Reconcile	Relapse	Require	Revoke	Rupture
Recondition	Relate	Requisition	Revolt	Rush
Reconstitute	Relax	Rescind	Revolutionize	Rust
Reconstruct	Relay	Rescue	Revolve	Rustle
Record	Release			

—S—

Sabotage	Sew	Slither	Spread	Strut
Sack	Shackle	Slobber	Spring	Stub
Sacrifice	Shade	Slop	Sprinkle	Study
Sadden	Shadow	Slosh	Sprint	Stuff
Saddle	Shaft	Slouch	Sprout	Stumble
Safeguard	Shag	Slow	Spur	Stump
Sag	Shake	Slug	Spurn	Stun
Sail	Shakeup	Slumber	Spurt	Stupefy
Salivate	Shall	Slump	Sputter	Stutter
Salute	Sham	Slur	Spy	Style
Salvage	Shamble	Smack	Squabble	Stylize
Sample	Shame	Small	Squander	Stymie
Sanction	Shanghai	Smart	Square	Subcontract
Sandbag	Shape	Smash	Squash	Subdivide
Sandblast	Share	Smear	Squat	Subdue

Sandpaper	Sharpen	Smell	Squawk	Subject
Sandwich	Shatter	Smile	Squeak	Subjugate
Sap	Shave	Smirch	Squeal	Sublease
Sass	Shear	Smite	Squeeze	Sublet
Satiate	Shed	Smoke	Squelch	Submerge
Satirize	Shell	Smolder	Squint	Submit
Satisfy	Shellac	Smooth	Squire	Subordinate
Saturate	Shelter	Smother	Squirm	Subpoena
Saunter	Shelve	Smudge	Squirt	Subscribe
Sauté	Shield	Smuggle	Squish	Subside
Save	Shift	Snag	Stab	Subsidize
Savor	Shimmer	Snap	Stabilize	Subsist
Saw	Shimmy	Snare	Stack	Substantiate
Say	Shine	Snarl	Stage	Substitute
Scald	Ship	Snatch	Stagger	Subtract
Scale	Shirk	Sneak	Stagnate	Subvert
Scalp	Shiver	Sneer	Stain	Succeed
Scamper	Shock	Sneeze	Stake	Succor
Scan	Shoot	Snicker	Stalemate	Succumb
Scandalize	Shop	Sniff	Stalk	Suck
Scapegoat	Shore	Sniffle	Stall	Suckle
Scar	Shortchange	Snigger	Stammer	Sue
Scare	Shorten	Snip	Stamp	Suffer
Scat	Shoulder	Snitch	Stampede	Suffice
Scathe	Shout	Snivel	Stand	Suffocate
Scatter	Shove	Snooker	Standardize	Suffuse
Scavenge	Shovel	Snoop	Star	Sugarcoat
Schedule	Show	Snooze	Stare	Suggest
Scheme	Shower	Snore	Start	Suit
Schlep	Shred	Snort	Startle	Sulk
Schuss	Shriek	Snow	Starve	Sully
Scintillate	Shrink	Snub	Stash	Summarize
Scoff	Shrivel	Snuff	State	Summon
Scold	Shroud	Snuggle	Station	Sunbathe
Scoop	Shrug	Soak	Staunch	Sup
Scoot	Shuck	Soar	Stave	Supercharge
Scorch	Shudder	Sob	Stay	Superimpose
Score	Shuffle	Socialize	Steady	Superintend
Scorn	Shun	Sock	Steal	Supersede
Scour	Shut	Soften	Steam	Supervise

Scourge	Shutter	Soft-pedal	Steamroll	Supplant
Scout	Sicken	Soft-soap	Steer	Supplement
Scowl	Sidestep	Soil	Stem	Supplicate
Scram	Sidetrack	Solace	Step	Supply
Scramble	Siege	Solder	Stereotype	Support
Scrap	Sift	Solemnize	Sterilize	Suppose
Scrape	Sigh	Solicit	Stew	Suppress
Scratch	Sign	Solidify	Steward	Surcease
Scrawl	Signal	Solo	Stick	Surf
Scream	Signify	Solve	Stiffen	Surface
Screech	Silence	Soothe	Stifle	Surge
Screen	Simmer	Sop	Stigmatize	Surmise
Screw	Simper	Sort	Stimulate	Surmount
Scribble	Simplify	Sound	Sting	Surpass
Scrimmage	Simulate	Sour	Stink	Surprise
Scrimp	Sin	Sow	Stipulate	Surrender
Script	Sing	Spade	Stir	Surround
Scrounge	Singe	Span	Stitch	Survey
Scrub	Sink	Spank	Stock	Survive
Scrunch	Sip	Spar	Stockpile	Suspect
Scrutinize	Sissify	Spare	Stoke	Suspend
Scuffle	Sit	Spark	Stomach	Sustain
Sculpt	Situate	Sparkle	Stomp	Swab
Scurry	Size	Spatter	Stone	Swaddle
Scuttle	Sizzle	Spawn	Stonewall	Swagger
Seal	Skate	Speak	Stoop	Swallow
Sear	Skedaddle	Spear	Stop	Swamp
Search	Sketch	Spearhead	Store	Swap
Seat	Skewer	Specialize	Storm	Swarm
Secede	Ski	Specify	Stow	Swat
Seclude	Skid	Speculate	Straddle	Swathe
Second	Skim	Speed	Strafe	Sway
Secrete	Skimp	Spell	Straggle	Swear
Secure	Skin	Spellbind	Straighten	Sweat
Sedate	Skip	Spend	Straightjacket	Sweep
Seduce	Skirmish	Spew	Strain	Sweeten
See	Skirt	Spice	Strand	Swell
Seed	Skulk	Spike	Strangle	Swelter
Seek	Skunk	Spill	Strap	Swerve
Seem	Skyrocket	Spin	Strategize	Swig

Seep	Slack	Spiral	Stray	Swill
Seethe	Slacken	Spite	Streak	Swim
Segregate	Slake	Splash	Stream	Swindle
Seize	Slam	Splice	Streamline	Swing
Select	Slander	Splinter	Strengthen	Swipe
Self-destruct	Slant	Split	Stress	Swish
Sell	Slap	Splurge	Stretch	Switch
Send	Slash	Spoil	Strew	Swivel
Sense	Slaughter	Sponge	Stride	Swoon
Sentence	Slay	Sponsor	Strike	Swoop
Separate	Sleep	Spoof	String	Symbolize
Sequester	Slice	Spook	Strip	Sympathize
Serenade	Slide	Spot	Strive	Synchronize
Serve	Slight	Spotlight	Stroke	Syncopate
Service	Sling	Spout	Stroll	Syndicate
Set	Slink	Sprain	Strong-arm	Synthesize
Settle	Slip	Sprawl	Structure	Systemize
Sever	Slit	Spray	Strong-arm	
			Structure	
			Struggle	

— T—

Table	Telegraph	Till	Tower	Trick
Tabulate	Telephone	Tilt	Trace	Trifle
Tack	Televise	Time	Track	Trigger
Tackle	Tell	Tinge	Trade	Trim
Tag	Temper	Tingle	Trail	Trip
Tail	Tempt	Tinker	Train	Triple
Tailgate	Tend	Tint	Traipse	Triumph
Tailor	Tender	Tip	Tramp	Trivialize
Taint	Terminate	Tipple	Trample	Trod
Take	Terrify	Tiptoe	Tranquilize	Troll
Takeoff	Terrorize	Tire	Transact	Trot
Talk	Test	Titillate	Transcend	Trouble
Tally	Testify	Titter	Transcribe	Troubleshoot
Tame	Tether	Toast	Transcribe	Trounce
Tamper	Thank	Toboggan	Transfer	Truck
Tan	Thaw	Toddle	Transfix	Trudge
Tangle	Theorize	Toe	Transform	Trump
Tango	Thicken	Toil	Transgress	Trumpet
Tank	Thieve	Tolerate	Translate	Truncate
Tantalize	Thin		Transmit	Trust

Tap	Think	Toll	Transmogrify	Try
Tape	Thirst	Tone	Transpire	Tuck
Taper	Thrash	Toot	Transplant	Tug
Tar	Threaten	Top	Transport	Tumble
Target	Thrill	Topple	Transpose	Tunnel
Tarnish	Thrive	Torch	Trap	Turn
Tarry	Throb	Torment	Trash	Tutor
Task	Throng	Torpedo	Traumatize	Tweak
Taste	Throttle	Torture	Travel	Tweet
Tattle	Throw	Toss	Traverse	Twinkle
Taunt	Thrust	Tote	Trawl	Twirl
Tax	Thump	Totter	Tread	Twist
Teach	Thunder	Touch	Treasure	Twitter
Team	Thwart	Tour	Treat	Two-time
Tear	Tick	Tousle	Trek	Type
Tease	Tickle	Tout	Tremble	Typify
Teem	Tie	Tow	Trespass	Tyrannize
Teeter	Tighten			

— U —

Ulcerate	Undergo	Unearth	Unmask	Unwrap
Umpire	Underline	Unfasten	Unnerve	Unzip
Unbend	Undermine	Unfetter	Unpack	Upbraid
Unbuckle	Underperform	Unfold	Unravel	Upchuck
Unburden	Underpin	Unfurl	Unroll	Update
Unbutton	Underrate	Unhand	Unscramble	Upgrade
Uncloak	Underscore	Unhinge	Unseal	Uphold
Uncork	Undersell	Unhook	Unseat	Uproot
Uncouple	Understand	Unify	Unsettle	Upset
Uncover	Understate	Unite	Unshackle	Upstage
Underachieve	Undertake	Unitize	Unsheathe	Urge
Underbid	Undervalue	Unleash	Untangle	Use
Undercharge	Underwrite	Unload	Untidy	Usher
Undercut	Undo	Unlock	Untie	Usurp
Underestimate	Undress	Unloose	Unveil	Utilize
Underexpose	Undulate	Unman	Unwind	Utter

— V —

Vacate	Vanish	Venerate	Victimize	Vocalize
Vacation	Vanquish	Vent	Vie	Vociferate
Vaccinate	Vaporize	Ventilate	View	Voice
Vacillate	Varnish	Venture	Vilify	Void
Vacuum	Vary	Verbalize	Vindicate	Volley

Vagrant	Vault	Verify	Violate	Volunteer
Validate	Vaunt	Vest	Visit	Vote
Value	Veer	Veto	Visualize	Vouch
Vamoose	Vegetate	Vex	Vitalize	Vouchsafe
Vamp	Veil	Vibrate	Vivify	Vow
Vandalize	Vend			

—W—

Wad	Warp	Weld	Wiggle	Wonder
Waddle	Warrant	Wend	Will	Woo
Wade	Wash	Wet	Wilt	Work
Wag	Waste	Whack	Win	Worm
Wage	Watch	Wheedle	Wince	Worry
Wager	Water	Wheeze	Wind	Worsen
Wait	Wave	Whet	Windsurf	Worship
Waive	Waver	Whiff	Wink	Wound
Wake	Wax	Whimper	Winnow	Wow
Waken	Waylay	Whine	Winterize	Wrangle
Wakeup	Weak	Whip	Wipe	Wrap
Walk	Weaken	Whipsaw	Wire	Wreck
Wallop	Wean	Whirl	Wiretap	Wrench
Wallow	Wear	Whisk	Wisecrack	Wrest
Waltz	Weather	Whisper	Wish	Wrestle
Wan	Weave	Whistle	Withdraw	Wriggle
Wander	Wed	Whitewash	Wither	Wring
Wane	Wedge	Whittle	Withhold	Wrinkle
Want	Weed	Whoop	Withstand	Write
War	Weep	Widen	Witness	Writhe
Warm	Weigh	Wield	Wobble	Wrong
Warn	Welcome			

—X—

X-ray

—Y—

Yak	Yawn	Yell	Yoke	Yowl
Yammer	Yap	Yelp	Yip	Yo-yo
Yank	Yearn	Yield	Yodel	

—Z—

Zap	Zigzag	Zipper	Zonk	Zoom
Zip	Zing			

APPENDIX E
ADJECTIVE ARCHIVE

— A —

Abaft	Accessible	Advanced	Aromatic	Attainable
Abandoned	Accidental	Advantaged	Arrant	Attendant
Aberrant	Accident-prone	Advantageous	Arresting	Attentive
Abhorrent	Acclimated	Adventuresome	Arrogant	Attractive
Abiding	Accommodated	Adventurous	Artful	Attuned
Abject	Accompanying	Adverse	Articulate	Atypical
Ablaze	Accomplished	Affectionate	Artificial	Audacious
Able	Accountable	Agonizing	Artistic	Audible
Able-bodied	Accurate	Alienated	Artless	August
Abnormal	Accursed	Aloof	Arty	Aural
Abominable	Accuse	Alterable	Ascendant	Auspicious
Aboriginal	Accustomed	Alternative	Ascetic	Austere
Abortive	Acetic	Amateurish	Ashamed	Authentic
Aboveboard	Acidic	Ambitious	Ashen	Authoritarian
Abrasive	Acoustic	Amenable	Ashore	Authoritative
Abreast	Acquisitive	Amiable	Asinine	Autocratic
Abridge	Acrid	Amusing	Askew	Automatic
Abroad	Acrimonious	Ancient	Asocial	Automotive
Abrupt	Acrobatic	Angelic	Aspiring	Autonomous
Absent	Active	Anguished	Assertive	Auxiliary
Absent-minded	Actual	Animated	Assiduous	Available
Absolute	Acute	Antagonistic	Assorted	Avant-garde
Absorbed	Adamant	Anxious	Assuaging	Avaricious
Absorbent	Adaptable	Approximate	Assuming	Average
Absorbing	Additional	Arbitrary	Assured	Averse
Abstemious	Additive	Arcane	Astir	Avid
Abstinent	Adept	Arch	Astonishing	Avowed
Abstract	Adequate	Archaic	Astounding	Awaiting
Abstracted	Adhesive	Archetypal	Astray	Awake
Abstruse	Adjacent	Arctic	Astringent	Aware
Absurd	Adjective	Ardent	Astronomical	Awash
Abundant	Adjunct	Arduous	Astute	Awesome
Abusive	Admirable	Arguable	Asymmetrical	Awestruck
Abutting	Admissible	Argumentative	Athletic	Awful
Abysmal	Adolescent	Arid	Atilt	Awkward

Academic	Adorable	Aristocratic	Atomic	Awry
Acceptable	Adroit	Armed	Atrocious	Axiomatic
Accepted	Adult			

— B —

Baby	Bedeviled	Bionic	Blushing	Brief
Backbreaking	Bedraggled	Bipartisan	Blusterous	Bright
Backhanded	Befitting	Bipolar	Blustery	Brilliant
Backup	Befuddled	Bird's-eye	Boastful	Brimming
Backward	Beggarly	Bitchy	Bodacious	Brisk
Bad	Begrudging	Biting	Bodily	Brittle
Bad-tempered	Beguiling	Bitter	Bogus	Broad
Baffling	Behemoth	Bittersweet	Bohemian	Broad-minded
Baggy	Behind	Bizarre	Boiling	Broken
Balanced	Beholden	Blah	Boisterous	Broken-hearted
Bald	Belated	Blamable	Bold	Brooding
Bald-faced	Beleaguered	Blameless	Boldfaced	Brotherly
Balding	Believable	Blameworthy	Bombastic	Brusque
Baleful	Bellicose	Bland	Bombed	Brutal
Balky	Belligerent	Blank	Bone-fide	Brutish
Ballistic	Belong	Blaring	Bonkers	Bubbling
Ballooning	Beloved	Blasé	Bonny	Bubbly
Balmy	Below	Blasphemous	Bookish	Bucolic
Banal	Bemused	Blasted	Booming	Buffoonish
Bang-up	Beneficent	Blatant	Boorish	Bulging
Bankable	Beneficial	Blazing	Bordering	Bulky
Bankrupt	Benevolent	Bleak	Boring	Bulletproof
Barbarian	Benighted	Bleary	Bossy	Bullheaded
Barbaric	Benign	Blessed	Bothersome	Bullish
Barbarous	Benignant	Blighted	Bound	Bumbling
Barbed	Benumbed	Blind	Boundless	Bumptious
Bare	Bereaved	Blinding	Bounteous	Bumpy
Bare-bones	Bereft	Blissful	Bountiful	Bungling
Barefaced	Berserk	Blistering	Bourgeois	Buoyant
Barefoot	Besetting	Blithe	Bracing	Burdened
Barehanded	Besides	Bloated	Brackish	Burdensome
Barren	Besotted	Block-headed	Brainless	Bureaucratic
Baseless	Bestial	Blonde	Brainy	Burgeoning
Bashful	Betrothed	Bloodcurdling	Brash	Burlesque
Basic	Better	Bloodthirsty	Brassy	Burly

Battered
Battle-scarred
Batty
Bawdy
Bearish

Beastly
Beauteous
Beautiful
Becoming
Bedazzled

Bedecked

Bevy
Bewildered
Bewildering
Bewitching
Bighearted

Bigoted
Bilateral
Bilingual
Bilious
Binding

Biodegradable

Bloody
Blooming
Bloviated
Blubbering
Blueblood

Blue-chip
Blue-collar
Blundering
Blunt
Blurred

Blurry

Bratty
Brave
Brawny
Brazen
Breakaway

Breakneck
Breakthrough
Breathless
Breathtaking
Breezy

Bribable

Burned-out
Burning
Bursting
Bush
Bushed

Bush-league
Businesslike
Bustling
Button-down
Buxom

Bygone

— C —

Cacophonic
Cadaverous
Cagey
Calamitous
Calculating

Callous
Calm
Calming
Calorific
Candid

Cannibalistic
Canny
Cantankerous
Capable
Capacious

Capricious
Captivating
Cardinal
Carefree
Careful

Careless
Carnal
Carnivorous
Casual
Cataclysmic

Catastrophic
Catching
Catchy
Categorical
Catty

Cheap
Checkered
Cheeky
Cheerful
Cheery

Cheesy
Cherished
Cherubic
Chic
Chipper

Chronic
Circumspect
Civilized
Clammy
Classic

Clownish
Clumsy
Cogent
Cognitive
Cognizant

Coherent
Comfortable
Comforting
Comingled
Commendable

Committed
Commodious
Common
Commonplace
Concentrated

Conceptual
Concerned
Concerted
Conciliatory
Concise

Conclusive
Concocted
Concomitant
Concrete
Concurrent

Condensed
Condescending
Conditional
Conducive
Confederate

Confetti
Confident
Confidential
Confined
Confining

Confirmed
Confiscatory
Conflicted
Conflicting
Confluent

Confoundedly
Confounding
Confrontational
Confused
Contented

Contentious
Contiguous
Continual
Continuous
Contraband

Contradictory
Contrary
Contrite
Contrived
Controversial

Convenient
Conventional
Conversant
Convertible
Convincing

Convivial
Convoluted
Convulsed
Convulsive
Cookie-cutter

Cool
Cooperative
Copacetic
Copious
Coquettish

Cordial
Corking
Corny
Corporal
Corporate

Crammed
Cramped
Cranky
Crashing
Crass

Craven
Crazed
Crazy
Creaky
Creative

Credible
Creditable
Credulous
Creepy
Crescent

Crestfallen
Criminal
Crippling
Crisp
Critical

Crooked
Cross
Crotchety
Crowd
Crowded

Crucial
Crude
Cruel
Crummy
Crushing

Caustic	Communal	Confusing	Corpulent	Cryptic
Cautions	Communicative	Congenial	Correctable	Crystal
Cavalier	Compact	Congruous	Corrective	Crystalline
Cavernous	Comparable	Conjectural	Corresponding	Cuckoo
Ceaseless	Comparative	Conjoint	Corrigible	Cuddly
Celebrated	Compassionate	Conjugal	Corrosive	Culinary
Celestial	Compatible	Conniving	Corrupt	Culpable
Censorious	Compelling	Conscientious	Corruptible	Cultivated
Censurable	Competent	Conscionable	Cosmic	Cultured
Central	Competitive	Conscious	Cosmopolitan	Cumbersome
Cerebral	Complacent	Consecutive	Costly	Cumulative
Ceremonial	Complaisant	Consequential	Counterfeit	Cunning
Ceremonious	Complete	Conservative	Countless	Curable
Certain	Complex	Considerable	Countrified	Curious
Chafing	Compliant	Considerate	Countrywide	Curly
Chagrined	Complicated	Consistent	Courageous	Current
Chalky	Complimentary	Consonant	Courteous	Cursed
Challenging	Composed	Conspicuous	Covert	Cursory
Chancy	Composite	Constant	Covetous	Curt
Changeable	Compound	Constituent	Cowardly	Curvaceous
Changeless	Compounded	Constructive	Coy	Cushy
Chaotic	Comprehensive	Consummate	Cozy	Custodial
Characteristic	Compressed	Contagious	Crabby	Customary
Charismatic	Compromising	Contaminated	Cracked	Cute
Charitable	Compulsive	Contemporary	Crackerjack	Cutthroat
Charming	Concealed	Contemptible	Crafty	Cutting
Chaste	Conceited	Contemptuous	Craggy	Cynical
Chatty	Conceivable	Content	Crusty	

— D —

Daffy	Definite	Dicey	Disillusioned	Domesticated
Daft	Definitive	Dictatorial	Disinclined	Dominant
Dainty	Deft	Didactic	Disingenuous	Dominating
Damaging	Defunct	Different	Disinterested	Domineering
Damnable	Defying	Difficult	Disjointed	Done
Damned	Degenerate	Diffusive	Disliked	Doomed
Damp	Degrading	Digital	Disloyal	Dopey
Dandy	Deliberate	Dignified	Dismal	Dormant
Dangerous	Delicate	Dilapidated	Dismaying	Doting
Dank	Delightful	Dilatory	Dismissive	Dotty

Dapper	Delirious	Diligent	Disobedient	Double
Dappled	Deluded	Diluted	Disorderly	Double-barreled
Daredevil	Demanding	Dim	Disoriented	Doubtful
Daring	Democratic	Diminished	Disparaging	Doughty
Dark	Demoniac	Diminutive	Disparate	Dour
Darling	Demonstrable	Dimwitted	Dispensable	Dowdy
Dashing	Demonstrative	Dingy	Dispirited	Down
Dashy	Dense	Dinky	Disposed	Downbeat
Dastardly	Dependable	Diplomatic	Disputatious	Downcast
Dated	Dependent	Dippy	Disputed	Downhearted
Daunting	Depleted	Dire	Disreputable	Downright
Dauntless	Depraved	Direful	Disrespectful	Down-to-earth
Dazed	Depressed	Dirt-cheap	Disruptive	Downtrodden
Dazzling	Depressing	Dirty	Dissatisfied	Drab
Dead	Derivative	Disabled	Dissimilar	Draconian
Deadly	Derogatory	Disadvantaged	Dissipated	Drafty
Dead-pan	Descending	Disaffected	Dissolute	Dramatic
Deaf	Descriptive	Disagreeable	Dissonant	Drastic
Deafening	Deserted	Disappointed	Distant	Drawn
Dear	Deserved	Disappointing	Distasteful	Dreaded
Dearth	Deserving	Disarming	Distended	Dreadful
Deathless	Designing	Disastrous	Distinct	Dreamy
Deathly	Desirable	Discernable	Distinctive	Dreary
Debased	Desirous	Discerning	Distinguishable	Drenching
Debatable	Desolate	Disciplined	Distinguished	Dressy
Debauched	Despairing	Discombobulated	Distinguishing	Dripping
Debilitated	Desperate	Disconcerted	Distorted	Driven
Debilitating	Despicable	Disconcerting	Distracted	Droll
Debonair	Despondent	Disconnected	Distracting	Droopy
Decadent	Despotic	Disconsolate	Distraught	Drowsy
Decayed	Destined	Discontented	Distress	Drunk
Deceased	Destitute	Discordant	Distressed	Drunken
Deceitful	Destructive	Discouraged	Distressing	Dubious
Decent	Detached	Discouraging	Distrustful	Ducky
Deceptive	Detailed	Discourteous	Disturbing	Dull
Decided	Deteriorated	Discreditable	Ditsy	Dumb
Decisive	Determined	Discreet	Divergent	Dumbfounded
Decorative	Detestable	Discrepant	Diverse	Dumbfounding
Decorous	Detrimental	Discrete	Diversified	Dumpy
Decrepit	Devastating	Discriminating	Diverting	Duplicate

Dedicated
Deep
Deep-seated
Defamatory
Defeated

Deviant
Devilish
Devine
Devious
Devoid

Disdainful
Diseased
Disenchanted
Disfigured
Disgraced

Divine
Divisive
Dizzy
Docile
Doctored

Duplicated
Duplicitous
Durable
Dusky
Dusty

Defective
Defenseless
Defensible
Defensive
Deferential

Devoted
Devout
Dewy
Dexterous
Diabolic

Disgraceful
Disgruntled
Disguised
Disgusting
Disheartened

Doctrinaire
Doddering
Dogged
Dogmatic
Doleful

Dutiful
Dwarfish
Dwindling
Dying
Dynamic

Defiant
Deficient

Diabolical
Diametrical

Dishonest
Dishonorable

Domestic
Domestic

Dysfunctional

— E —

Eager
Eagle-eyed
Early
Earnest
Earsplitting

Elephantine
Elevated
Elfish
Eligible
Embattled

Enterprising
Entertaining
Enthralling
Enthusiastic
Enticing

Ethereal
Ethical
Ethnic
Euphonious
Euphoric

Exiguous
Existent
Existing
Exorbitant
Exotic

Earthshaking
Earthy
Easy
Easygoing
Ebullient

Empathetic
Emphatic
Empirical
Employable
Empowered

Entire
Entranced
Entrancing
Entrapped
Entrenched

Evanescent
Evasive
Even
Evenhanded
Eventful

Expanded
Expansive
Expectant
Expecting
Expedient

Eccentric
Eclectic
Ecological
Economical
Ecstatic

Empty
Empty-headed
Enamored
Enchanting
Encouraging

Entrepreneurial
Enumerated
Enunciated
Envenomed
Enviable

Everlasting
Everyday
Evident
Evil
Evil-eyed

Expeditious
Expendable
Expensive
Experienced
Experimental

Edgy
Edible
Edifying
Educated
Educational

Encumbered
Encyclopedic
Endangered
Endearing
Endless

Envious
Environmental
Ephemeral
Epic
Epicurean

Evil-minded
Eviscerating
Evocative
Evolutionary
Evolving

Expert
Expired
Explainable
Explanatory
Explicable

Eerie
Effective
Effectual
Effeminate
Effervescent

Endurable
Enduring
Energetic
Energized
Enervated

Epidemic
Epigrammatic
Episodic
Epochal
Equable

Exact
Exacting
Exaggerated
Exalted
Exasperated

Explicit
Exploitable
Explosive
Exponential
Express

Expressive	Elementary	Entail	Eternal	Exquisite
Effete	Enfeebled	Equal	Exasperating	Extant
Efficacious	Engaged	Equitable	Excavated	Extemporaneous
Efficient	Engaging	Equivalent	Excellent	Extended
Effortless	Engrossed	Equivocal	Exceptional	Extensive
Effulgent	Engrossing	Equivocated	Excess	Extenuating
Effusive	Enhanced	Erect	Excessive	Exterior
Egalitarian	Enigmatic	Ergo	Excitable	External
Egocentric	Enjoyable	Ernest	Excited	Extinct
Egomaniacal	Enlarged	Erotic	Exciting	Extortionate
Egotistical	Enlightened	Errant	Exclusive	Extra
Egregious	Enlightening	Erratic	Excruciating	Extralegal
Elaborate	Enlivened	Erroneous	Excusable	Extraneous
Elastic	Enlivening	Ersatz	Executive	Extraordinary
Elated	Enmeshed	Erstwhile	Exemplary	Extravagant
Elective	Ennobling	Erudite	Exempt	Extreme
Electric	Enormous	Escalated	Exercised	Extrinsic
Electrified	Enough	Esoteric	Exhausted	Extroverted
Electrifying	Enraged	Essential	Exhausting	Exuberant
Electronic	Enraptured	Established	Exhaustive	Exultant
Elegant	Enriched	Esteemed	Exhilarated	Eye-opening
Elegiac	Enshrined	Estimable	Exhilarating	
Elemental	Ensuing	Estranged	Exigent	

— F —

Fabled	Favorable	Fiscal	Following	Freehand
Fabulous	Favored	Fishy	Fond	Freewheeling
Facetious	Favorite	Fit	Foolhardy	Free-will
Facile	Fawning	Fitful	Foolish	Frenetic
Factious	Fearful	Fitting	Foolproof	Frenzied
Factual	Fearless	Fixed	Footloose	Frequent
Faddish	Fearsome	Fizzy	Foppish	Fresh
Fagged	Feasible	Flabbergasted	Forbearing	Fretful
Faint	Featherbrained	Flabbergasting	Forbidding	Friendless
Fainthearted	Featured	Flabby	Forced	Friendly
Fair	Feckless	Flaccid	Forceful	Frightening
Fair-minded	Federal	Flagging	Forcible	Frightful
Fair-spoken	Feeble	Flagrant	Foreboding	Frigid
Fair-weather	Feeble-minded	Flaky	Foregoing	Frilly
Faithful	Feisty	Flamboyant	Foregone	Frisky

Fake	Felicitous	Flaming	Forehanded	Frivolous
Fallacious	Felonious	Flammable	Foreign	Frolicsome
Fallible	Feminine	Flappable	Foremost	Frosty
Fallow	Feral	Flashy	Foreseeable	Frowsy
False	Ferocious	Flat-footed	Forgetful	Frozen
Faltering	Fertile	Flat-out	Forgiving	Frugal
Famed	Fervent	Flattered	Forgone	Fruitful
Familiar	Festering	Flattering	Forgotten	Fruitless
Famished	Festive	Flawed	Forlorn	Frumpy
Famous	Fetching	Flawless	Formal	Frustrated
Fanatic	Fetid	Fleet	Formative	Frustrating
Fanatical	Feudal	Fleet-footed	Former	Fugitive
Fanciful	Feverish	Fleeting	Formidable	Full-bodied
Fancy	Few	Fleshy	Formless	Full-fledged
Fantastic	Fewer	Flexible	Forthcoming	Full-grown
Farcical	Fiat	Flickering	Forthright	Fulsome
Far-fetched	Fickle	Flighty	Fortified	Functional
Far-flung	Fictional	Flimflam	Fortuitous	Fundamental
Far-off	Fictitious	Flimsy	Fortunate	Funereal
Far-out	Fictive	Flinty	Forward	Funky
Far-reaching	Fidgety	Flip	Foul	Funny
Farseeing	Fiendish	Flippant	Founder	Furious
Farsighted	Fierce	Flirtatious	Foxy	Furry
Farthest	Fiery	Floppy	Fractious	Furtive
Fascinated	Figurative	Floral	Fragile	Fussy
Fascinating	Filmy	Florid	Fragrant	Futile
Fashionable	Filtered	Flourishing	Frail	Future
Fastidious	Filthy	Flowery	Frame	Fuzzy
Fatal	Final	Fluctuating	Frangible	Fallacious
Fated	Financial	Fluent	Frank	Far-fetched
Fateful	Fine	Fluffy	Frantic	Fathomable
Fatherly	Finical	Fluid	Fraternal	Fishy
Fatigued	Finicky	Fluky	Fraudulent	Flawed
Fatiguing	Finished	Flush	Fraught	Flawless
Fatty	Finite	Flustering	Frayed	Flimsy
Fatuous	Fireproof	Fly-by-night	Frazzled	Foreordained
Faultfinding	Firm	Flying	Freakish	Fruitless
Faultless	First-class	Foamy	Freaky	Frustrating
Faulty	Firsthand	Foggy	Free	Futile
Faux	First-rate	Folksy		

— G —

Gabby	Germane	Glorified	Grandiose	Grounded
Gainful	Ghastly	Glorious	Graphic	Groundless
Galactic	Ghostly	Glossy	Grasping	Groveling
Gallant	Ghoulish	Glowing	Grateful	Growing
Galling	Giant	Glum	Gratified	Grown
Galore	Giddy	Gluttonous	Gratifying	Grubby
Galvanizing	Gifted	Gnarly	Grating	Grudging
Game	Gigantic	Golden	Gratis	Grueling
Gamey	Giggly	Gold-plated	Gratuitous	Gruesome
Gangling	Gilded	Good	Grave	Gruff
Gardening	Gilt-edged	Good-hearted	Greasy	Grumpy
Gargantuan	Gimpy	Good-humored	Great	Grungy
Garish	Gingerly	Good-looking	Great-hearted	Guaranteed
Garrulous	Girlish	Good-natured	Greedy	Guarded
Gaseous	Given	Good-tempered	Gregarious	Guided
Gassy	Glacial	Gooey	Grief-stricken	Guileful
Gauche	Glad	Goofy	Grievous	Guileless
Gaudy	Gladdening	Gorgeous	Grim	Guilt-ridden
Gaunt	Gladsome	Gory	Grimy	Guilty
Gawky	Glamorous	Gossamer	Grinding	Gullible
Geeky	Glaring	Gossipy	Gripping	Gung ho
General	Gleeful	Gothic	Grisly	Gun-shy
Generic	Glib	Gourmet	Gritty	Gussy
Generous	Glimmering	Graceful	Grizzled	Gusty
Genial	Glistening	Graceless	Groggy	Gutless
Genteel	Glittering	Gracious	Groovy	Gutsy
Gentle	Glittery	Gradual	Gross	Gutty
Genuine	Glitzy	Grand	Grotesque	Gymnastic
Geriatric	Gloomy	Grandiloquent	Grouchy	

— H —

Habitable	Haywire	Helter-skelter	Hoary	Hourly
Habitual	Hazardous	Henpecked	Hobbled	Housebound
Hackneyed	Hazy	Herbivorous	Hoggish	Housebroken
Haggard	Headlong	Herculean	Ho-hum	Hovering
Hair-rising	Head-on	Hereditary	Hollow	Huffy
Hair-splitting	Headstrong	Heretic	Holy	Huge
Halcyon	Heady	Heretical	Homeless	Hulking
Half-hearted	Healthful	Heroic	Homely	Human
Half-witted	Healthy	Hesitant	Homemade	Humane
Hallowed	Heartbreaking	Heterogeneous	Homesick	Humanitarian

Handsome	Heartbroken	Hidden	Homespun	Humble
Handy	Heartening	Hideous	Homey	Humdrum
Hangdog	Heartfelt	High	Homicidal	Humid
Haphazard	Heartily	Highborn	Homogeneous	Humiliated
Hard-bitten	Heartless	Highbrow	Honest	Humiliating
Hardcore	Heartrending	High-class	Honeyed	Humming
Hardened	Heartsick	Highfalutin	Honky-tonk	Humongous
Hardheaded	Heartwarming	High-grade	Honorable	Humorous
Hardhearted	Hearty	Highhanded	Honorary	Humungous
Hard-hitting	Heated	High-hat	Honored	Hungry
Hardnosed	Heavenly	High-level	Honorific	Hunky-dory
Hard-pressed	Heavy	High-minded	Hooked	Hurried
Hardworking	Heavy-duty	High-pressure	Hopeful	Hurt
Hardy	Heavy-handed	High-profile	Hopeless	Hurtful
Harebrained	Hectic	High-rise	Horrendous	Hushed
Harmful	Hedonistic	High-spirited	Horrible	Husky
Harmless	Heedful	High-strung	Horrid	Hygienic
Harmonious	Heedless	Hilarious	Horrific	Hyper
Harrowing	Hefty	Hindmost	Horrified	Hyperactive
Harsh	Heightened	Hip	Horrifying	Hypercritical
Hasty	Heinous	Historic	Hospitable	Hypersensitive
Hateful	Hell-bent	Historical	Hostile	Hypnotic
Haughty	Hellish	Histrionic	Hot-blooded	Hypocritical
Haunted	Helpful	Hit-or-miss	Hotheaded	Hypothetical
Haunting	Helpless	Hoarse	Hot-tempered	Hysterical
Hawkish				

— I —

Icky	Impish	Indecipherable	Ingenious	Interior
Icy	Implacable	Indecisive	Inglorious	Intermediary
Ideal	Implausible	Indecorous	Ingrained	Intermediate
Idealistic	Implicit	Indefatigable	Ingratiating	Interminable
Identical	Implied	Indefensible	Inhabitable	Intermittent
Idiosyncratic	Impolite	Indefinable	Inharmonious	Internal
Idiotic	Impolitic	Indefinite	Inherent	International
Idle	Imponderable	Indelible	Inhibited	Internecine
Idolatrous	Importable	Indelicate	Inhuman	Interpersonal
Idyllic	Important	Independent	Inhumane	Interpolate
Iffy	Importune	In-depth	Inimical	Interpret
Ignoble	Imposing	Indescribable	Inimitable	Interpretive
Ignominious	Impossible	Indestructible	Iniquitous	Interstellar
Ignorant	Impotent	Indeterminate	Initial	Intimate
Ill	Impoverished	Indicative	Injudicious	Intimidate

Ill-advised	Impractical	Indifferent	Injurious	Intimidating
Ill-bred	Imprecise	Indigenous	Inky	Intolerable
Ill-disposed	Impregnable	Indigent	Innate	Intolerant
Illegal	Impressionable	Indignant	Inner	Intoxicated
Illegible	Impressive	Indirect	Innermost	Intractable
Illegitimate	Improbable	Indiscreet	Innocent	Intramural
Ill-fated	Impromptu	Indiscriminate	Innocuous	Intransigent
Ill-founded	Improper	Indiscriminately	Innovative	Intrepid
Ill-humored	Improved	Indispensible	Innumerable	Intricate
Illiberal	Improvident	Indisposed	Inoffensive	Intriguing
Illicit	Improvised	Indisputable	Inoperable	Intrinsic
Illiterate	Imprudent	Indistinct	Inoperative	Introductory
Ill-mannered	Impulsive	Indistinguishable	Inopportune	Introspective
Ill-natured	Impure	Individual	Inordinate	Introverted
Illogical	Inaccessible	Indolent	Inquisitive	Intruding
Ill-starred	Inaccurate	Indomitable	Insane	Intrusive
Ill-suited	Inactive	Indubitable	Insanitary	Intuitive
Ill-tempered	Inadequate	Indulgent	Insatiable	Inundated
Ill-timed	Inadvertent	Industrial	Inscrutable	Inured
Illuminated	Inalienable	Industrious	Insecure	Invalid
Illuminating	Inane	Inebriated	Insensible	Invaluable
Illusory	Inappreciable	Ineffable	Insensitive	Invariable
Illustrative	Inappropriate	Ineffective	Inseparable	Invasive
Illustrious	Inapt	Inefficient	Insidious	Inventive
Imaginable	Inarticulate	Inelastic	Insightful	Inverse
Imaginary	Inattentive	Inelegant	Insignificant	Inveterate
Imaginative	Inaudible	Ineligible	Insincere	Invidious
Imbecilic	Inauspicious	Inept	Insinuating	Invigorating
Imitation	Inauthentic	Inequitable	Insipid	Invincible
Imitative	Inborn	Inert	Insipient	Inviolable
Immaculate	Incalculable	Inescapable	Insistent	Inviolate
Immanent	Incandescent	Inevitable	Insolent	Invisible
Immaterial	Incapable	Inexact	Insoluble	Inviting
Immature	Incapacitated	Inexcusable	Insolvent	Involuntary
Immeasurable	Incautious	Inexhaustible	Insouciant	Involved
Immediate	Incendiary	Inexorable	Inspired	Invulnerable
Immense	Incensed	Inexpedient	Inspiring	Irascible
Imminent	Incessant	Inexpensive	Instable	Irate
Immobile	Incidental	Inexperienced	Instant	Iridescent
Immoderate	Incisive	Inexpert	Instantaneous	Irksome

Immodest	Inclement	Inexplicable	Instinctive	Ironclad
Immoral	Inclined	Inexpressible	Institutional	Ironfisted
Immortal	Inclusive	Inexpressive	Instructive	Ironic
Immovable	Incognizant	Inextinguishable	Instrumental	Ironical
Immune	Incoherent	Inextricable	Insubordinate	Irrational
Immutable	Incomparable	Infallible	Insubordinate	Irreconcilable
Impacted	Incompatible	Infamous	Insubstantial	Irrecoverable
Impaired	Incompetent	Infant	Insufferable	Irredeemable
Impart	Incomplete	Infantile	Insufficient	Irrefutable
Impartial	Incomprehensible	Infatuated	Insular	Irregular
Impassable	Inconceivable	Infected	Insulated	Irrelevant
Impassioned	Inconclusive	Infectious	Insulting	Irremovable
Impassive	Incongruent	Infective	Insuperable	Irreparable
Impatient	Incongruous	Infelicitous	Insupportable	Irrepressible
Impeccable	Inconsequential	Inferior	Insurgent	Irreproachable
Impecunious	Inconsiderable	Infernal	Insurmountable	Irresistible
Impelling	Inconsiderate	Infertile	Intact	Irresolute
Impending	Inconsistent	Infested	Intangible	Irrespective
Impenetrable	Inconsolable	Infinite	Integral	Irresponsible
Impenitent	Inconspicuous	Infinitesimal	Intellectual	Irretrievable
Imperative	Incontestable	Infirm	Intelligent	Irreverent
Imperceptible	Inconvenient	Inflamed	Intelligible	Irreversible
Imperfect	Incorporated	Inflammable	Intemperate	Irrevocable
Imperial	Incorrect	Inflammatory	Intended	Irritable
Imperiling	Incorrigible	Inflated	Intense	Irritant
Imperious	Incredible	Inflexible	Intensified	Irritated
Imperishable	Incredulous	Influential	Intensive	Irritating
Impermanent	Incremental	Informal	Intent	Isolated
Impersonal	Incriminating	Informative	Intentional	Italic
Impertinent	Incumbent	Informed	Interactive	Itchy
Imperturbable	Incurable	Infrequent	Interested	Iterate
Impervious	Indebted	Infuriated	Interesting	Itinerant
Impetuous	Indecent	Infuriating		

— J—

Jaded	Jerkwater	Jobless	Joyful	Jumbled
Jagged	Jerky	Jocular	Joyless	Jumbo
Jammed	Jerrybuilt	Jocund	Joyous	Jumpy
Jam-packed	Jet fueled	Joint	Jubilant	Junior
Jarring	Jet-propelled	Joking	Judgmental	Junky

Jaundiced
Jaunty
Jazzy
Jealous
Jeopardizing

Jim-dandy
Jingoistic
Jinxed
Jittery

Jolly
Jolting
Joshing
Jovial

Judicial
Judicious
Jugular
Juicy

Just
Justifiable
Justified
Juvenile

— K —

Kamikaze
Kaput
Keen
Key
Khaki

Killing
Kind
Kind-hearted
Kindly
Kindred

Kinky
Kissable
Kitschy
Kittenish
Kleptomaniac

Knavish
Knee deep
Knightly
Knobby
Knockabout

Knockout
Knotty
Knowing
Knowledgeable
Knuckledragging

Kicky
Kidding
Killer

Kingly
King-size

Klutzy
Knavery

Knockabout
Knock-kneed

Kooky
Kosher

— L —

Labored
Laborious
Labyrinthine
Lacerated
Lachrymal

Lawbreaking
Lawful
Lawless
Lax
Lazy

Liable
Libelous
Liberal
Liberated
Liberating

Literate
Lithe
Lithesome
Litigious
Livable

Lovelorn
Lacy
Lovely
Lovesick
Loving

Lachrymose
Lackadaisical
Lacking
Lackluster
Laconic

Lead
Leaded
Leaden
Leading
Leafy

Libertine
Libidinous
Licensed
Licentious
Licit

Live
Lively
Livid
Living
Loaded

Low
Low grade
Low key
Lowborn
Lowdown

Laden
Ladylike
Laggard
Laid-back
Lambent

Leaky
Lean
Leaning
Learned
Least

Lickety-split
Lifeless
Lifelike
Life-size
Light

Loath
Loathsome
Local
Located
Loco

Low-end
Lower
Low-key
Lowly
Low-pressure

Lame
Lamentable
Lamented
Landlocked
Languid

Leathery
Lecherous
Leery
Leeward
Left

Light-fingered
Light-footed
Lightheaded
Lighthearted
Lightning

Locomotive
Loftier
Lofty
Logical
Logy

Loyal
Lucent
Lucid
Luckless
Lucky

Languishing
Lanky
Lantern-jawed
Lapsed
Larcenous

Left-handed
Leftist
Left-wing
Legal
Legalistic

Lightweight
Likable
Like
Likely
Like-minded

Lone
Lonely
Lonesome
Long
Long-lived

Lucrative
Ludicrous
Lugubrious
Lukewarm
Lulling

Large	Legendary	Lilliputian	Long-range	Lumbering
Large-scale	Leggy	Lilly-livered	Long-standing	Luminous
Largish	Legible	Limber	Longwinded	Lumpish
Lascivious	Legislative	Limited	Loony	Lumpy
Last	Legitimate	Limiting	Looped	Lunar
Lasting	Leisurely	Limitless	Loopy	Lunatic
Late	Lengthy	Limp	Loose	Lurid
Latent	Lenient	Limpid	Lopsided	Lurking
Lateral	Less	Linear	Loquacious	Luscious
Latter	Lesser	Linguistic	Lordly	Lush
Laud	Lethal	Linked	Lost	Lustful
Laudable	Lethargic	Lionhearted	Loud	Lustrous
Laudatory	Lettered	Lippy	Loudmouthed	Lusty
Laughable	Letter-perfect	Liquid	Lousy	Luxurious
Laughing	Level	Lissome	Loutish	Lynx-eyed
Lavish	Levelheaded	Listless	Lovable	Lyric
Law-abiding	Lewd	Literal	Loveless	Lyrical

— M —

Macabre	Marginal	Melodic	Miscellaneous	Mortifying
Machiavellian	Marine	Melodious	Mischievous	Moth-eaten
Macho	Marital	Melodramatic	Miserable	Motionless
Mad	Maritime	Memorable	Miserly	Motivated
Madcap	Marked	Memorial	Misguided	Motivating
Maddening	Marketable	Mendacious	Misleading	Motivational
Magic	Married	Misspent	Misshapen	Motley
Magical	Marshy	Mistaken	Missing	Mottled
Magisterial	Martial	Menial	Mistrustful	Mountainous
Magnanimous	Marvelous	Mental	Misty	Mournful
Magnetic	Masculine	Mercenary	Misunderstood	Mousy
Magnificent	Masked	Merciful	Mixed	Mouthwatering
Mainstream	Masochistic	Merciless	Mixed-up	Mouthy
Majestic	Massive	Mercurial	Mobile	Movable
Major	Masterful	Meretricious	Mock	Moving
Makeshift	Matchless	Meritorious	Model	Mucky
Maladjusted	Material	Merry	Moderate	Muddled
Maladroit	Materialistic	Mesmerized	Modern	Muddleheaded
Malapropos	Maternal	Messy	Modest	Muddy
Malcontent	Mathematical	Metaphorical	Modified	Muggy

Maleficent
Malevolent
Malicious
Malignant
Malleable

Malnourished
Malodorous
Mammoth
Manageable
Managerial

Mandatory
Mandatory
Maneuverable
Manful
Mangy

Maniac
Maniacal
Manic
Manifest
Manifold

Manipulative
Manly
Mannered
Mannerly
Manual

Many
Marauding

Matter-of-fact
Mature
Maudlin
Maverick
Mawkish

Maximal
Maximum
Meager
Mean
Meandering

Meaningful
Meaningless
Mean-spirited
Measly
Measurable

Measured
Meaty
Mechanical
Meddlesome
Medical

Mediocre
Medium
Meek
Melancholic
Mellifluent

Mellifluous
Mellow

Meteoric
Methodical
Meticulous
Metropolitan
Mettlesome

Microscopic
Midcourse
Middling
Midway
Mighty

Migrant
Mild
Militant
Military
Mind-blowing

Mind-boggling
Mindful
Mindless
Mingled
Miniature

Miniscule
Minor
Minute
Miraculous
Mirthful

Mirthless
Misbegotten

Modish
Moist
Moldy
Mollifying
Momentarily

Momentary
Momentous
Monetary
Moneyed
Mongrel

Monolithic
Monopolistic
Monotonous
Monster
Monstrous

Monumental
Moody
Moonlit
Moonstruck
Moot

Moral
Morbid
Mordant
Moribund
Moronic

Morose
Mortal

Mulish
Multifaceted
Multifarious
Multiple
Multitude

Multitudinous
Mum
Mundane
Munificent
Murderous

Murky
Muscle-bound
Muscular
Mushy
Musical

Musing
Musty
Mutant
Mute
Mutilate

Mutinous
Mutual
Myopic
Mysterious
Mystical

Mystifying
Mythical

— N —

Nagging
Naïve
Naked
Nameless
Napping

Narcissistic
Narrow
Narrow-minded
Nascent
Nasty

Needless
Needy
Nefarious
Negative
Neglected

Negligent
Negligible
Negotiable
Neighbor
Neighboring

Newfangled
Newsworthy
Newsy
Next
Nice

Nifty
Nigh
Nimble
Nippy
Nit-picking

Noncombustible
Noncommittal
Noncompliant
Nonconflicting
Nonconforming

Nonconformist
Noncontroversial
Nondescript
Nondestructive
Nonessential

Nonproductive
Nonprofessional
Nonprofit
Nonrealistic
Nonrenewable

Nonsensical
Nonstop
Nonviolent
Normal
Nostalgic

Natal	Neighborly	Noble	Nonetheless	Notable
National	Neither	Nocturnal	Nonexempt	Noted
Native	Nepotistic	Nodding	Nonexistent	Noticeable
Natty	Nerdy	No-fault	Nonfictional	Notorious
Natural	Nerve-racking	Noiseless	Nonflammable	Novel
Naughty	Nervous	Noisy	Nonfunctional	Noxious
Nauseating	Nervy	Nomadic	Nonfunctioning	Nubile
Nauseous	Nestle	Nominal	Nonmaterial	Nude
Nautical	Netting	Nonabrasive	Nonmoving	Numb
Navigable	Nettlesome	Nonaggressive	Nonnegotiable	Numbed
Neanderthal	Neurotic	Nonaligned	No-nonsense	Numerous
Nearsighted	Neutral	Nonbinding	Nonpareil	Nutritious
Neat	Never	Nonchalant	Nonpartisan	Nutty
Necessary	Nevertheless			

— O —

Oafish	Odoriferous	One-track	Oratorical	Out-of-date
Obdurate	Odorous	Ongoing	Orderly	Out-of-the-way
Obedient	Offbeat	Online	Ordinary	Outrageous
Obese	Off-color	Only	Organic	Outré
Obfuscating	Offended	Onward	Organized	Outright
Objectionable	Offensive	Opaque	Orgiastic	Outspoken
Objective	Offhand	Open	Oriental	Outstanding
Obligated	Official	Opened	Original	Outward
Obligatory	Officious	Open-ended	Ornamental	Outworn
Obliged	Offish	Open-handed	Ornate	Oval
Obliging	Off-limits	Open-hearted	Ornery	Overall
Oblique	Offshore	Open-minded	Orphan	Overarching
Oblivious	Offside	Operable	Orthodox	Overbearing
Obnoxious	Offstage	Operational	Orwellian	Overblown
Obscene	Off-the-wall	Operative	Ostensible	Overcast
Obscure	Oft	Opinionated	Ostensive	Overconfident
Obsequious	Often	Opportune	Ostentatious	Overdue
Observant	Oily	Opportunistic	Other	Overflowing
Obsessed	OK	Opposed	Otherworldly	Overjoyed
Obsessive	Old	Opposing	Otiose	Overmuch
Obsolescent	Olden	Opposite	Out-and-out	Overpowering
Obsolete	Old-fashioned	Oppressed	Outbound	Overqualified
Obstinate	Old-time	Oppressive	Outcast	Overrated
Obstreperous	Olfactory	Opprobrious	Outclassed	Overriding
Obstructive	Olympian	Optic	Outdated	Oversize

Obtainable	Ominous	Optical	Outdoor	Overt
Obtrusive	Omnipotent	Optimal	Outer	Over-the-top
Obtuse	Omnipresent	Optimistic	Outgoing	Overweening
Obvious	Omniscient	Optimum	Outlandish	Overweight
Occasional	Omnivorous	Optional	Outlawed	Overwhelming
Occult	Oncoming	Opulent	Outlying	Overwork
Odd	Onerous	Oracular	Outmoded	Overwrought
Oddball	One-sided	Oral	Out-of-bounds	Oxymoronic
Odious				

—P—

Pacific	Penniless	Pitiful	Precocious	Progressive
Pacifistic	Pensive	Pitiless	Preconceived	Prohibitive
Packed	Pent-up	Placid	Precursory	Prolific
Pagan	Penultimate	Planetary	Predatory	Prolonged
Painful	Penurious	Plastered	Predestined	Prominent
Painless	Peppy	Plastic	Predetermine	Promiscuous
Painstaking	Perceptible	Platinum	Predictable	Promising
Palatable	Perceptive	Platonic	Predisposed	Prompt
Palatial	Perchance	Plausible	Predominant	Promulgated
Pale	Peremptory	Playful	Preeminent	Prone
Palliative	Perennial	Pleasant	Preemptory	Pronounced
Pallid	Perfect	Pleased	Prefabricated	Proper
Palpable	Perfidious	Pleasing	Prefatory	Prophetic
Paltry	Perfunctory	Pleasurable	Preferable	Propitious
Pampered	Perilous	Plenteous	Preferential	Proportional
Pandemic	Periodic	Plentiful	Pregnable	Proportionate
Panicky	Periodical	Pliable	Pregnant	Proprietary
Panic-stricken	Peripheral	Pliant	Prehistoric	Prosaic
Panoramic	Perishable	Plodding	Prejudicial	Prospective
Parabolic	Perky	Plucky	Preliminary	Prosperous
Paradigmatic	Permanent	Plumb	Premature	Prostrate
Paradoxical	Permeable	Plundering	Premeditated	Prosy
Parallel	Permissible	Plural	Premier	Protective
Paralytic	Permissive	Plus	Preoccupied	Protracted
Paralyzing	Permitted	Plush	Preordained	Proud
Paramount	Pernicious	Poetic	Preparatory	Proven
Paranoid	Perpetual	Poignant	Prepared	Proverbial
Parasitic	Perplexed	Pointed	Preponderant	Provident
Parched	Perplexing	Pointless	Preposterous	Providential
Pardonable	Perquisite	Poised	Prerequisite	Provincial

Parliamentary	Persevering	Poisonous	Prescient	Provisional
Parochial	Persistent	Poky	Present	Provocative
Parsimonious	Persnickety	Polar	Presentable	Provoking
Partial	Personable	Polemical	Present-day	Prudent
Participative	Personal	Polished	Pressing	Prudish
Particular	Perspicacious	Polite	Prestigious	Prurient
Partisan	Perspicuous	Politic	Presumptive	Pseudo
Partly	Persuasive	Political	Presumptuous	Psychic
Passable	Pert	Polluted	Pretentious	Psychological
Passé	Pertinacious	Pompous	Pretty	Psychopathic
Passing	Pertinent	Ponderous	Prevailing	Psychosomatic
Passionate	Perturbed	Pontifical	Prevalent	Psychotic
Passive	Perturbing	Pooped	Prevaricating	Public
Past	Pervasive	Poor	Preventive	Public-spirited
Pastoral	Perverse	Popular	Previous	Puckish
Pasty	Perverted	Populous	Priceless	Pudgy
Patchy	Pervious	Porous	Prickly	Puerile
Patent	Pesky	Portable	Priggish	Puffy
Patented	Pessimistic	Portentous	Prim	Pugnacious
Pathetic	Petite	Portly	Primal	Pulse-quickening
Pathological	Petrified	Posh	Primary	Pumped
Patient	Petrifying	Positive	Prime	Punchy
Patriotic	Petty	Possessed	Primitive	Punctilious
Patronizing	Petulant	Possessive	Primordial	Punctual
Paunchy	Phenomenal	Possible	Princely	Pungent
Payable	Philanthropic	Posterior	Principal	Punishing
Peaceable	Philosophical	Postgraduate	Principled	Punitive
Peaceful	Phlegmatic	Posthumous	Prior	Puny
Peachy	Phony	Potent	Pristine	Pure
Peaked	Photogenic	Potential	Private	Purebred
Peculiar	Physical	Potty	Privileged	Purified
Pecuniary	Picayune	Poverty-stricken	Probable	Puritan
Pedagogic	Picky	Powerful	Problematic	Puritanical
Pedantic	Pictorial	Powerless	Procedural	Purple
Pedestrian	Picturesque	Practicable	Pro-choice	Purportedly
Pedigreed	Piecemeal	Practical	Prodigious	Purposeful
Peerless	Piercing	Practiced	Productive	Purposeless
Peevish	Pigheaded	Pragmatic	Profane	Pushy
Pejorative	Pioneering	Praiseworthy	Professional	Putrid
Penal	Pious	Precarious	Proficient	Puzzling

Pending
Penetrable
Penetrating
Penitent

Piquant
Pitch-black
Piteous
Pithy

Precedent
Precious
Precipitous
Precise

Profitable
Profligate
Profound
Profuse

Pygmy
Pyrotechnical
Pyrrhic

— Q —

Quadrilateral
Quaint
Quaking
Quaky
Qualified

Quantitative
Quarrelsome
Quasi
Queasy
Queen-size

Querulous
Questionable
Questioning
Quibbling
Quick

Quick-witted
Quiescent
Quiet
Quieting
Quintessential

Quirky
Quit
Quivering
Quixotic
Quizzical

Qualitative
Qualmish

Queer
Querulous

Quick-tempered

Quintuple

Quotable

— R —

Rabid
Rackety
Racking
Racy
Radiant

Ravaged
Ravenous
Raving
Ravishing
Raw

Representative
Reproachable
Reprobate
Reproductive
Republican

Revengeful
Reverberating
Reverent
Reverential
Reverse

Robust
Rock-ribbed
Rocky
Rogue
Roguish

Radical
Raffish
Ragged
Raggedy
Raging

Raw-boned
Reachable
Reactionary
Reactive
Ready

Repugnant
Repulsive
Reputable
Reputable
Reputed

Reviling
Revived
Reviving
Revolting
Revolutionary

Roiled
Rollicking
Roly-poly
Romantic
Roomy

Rainy
Raised
Rakish
Rakishly
Rambling

Ready-made
Real
Relative
Relaxed
Relaxing

Required
Requisite
Resentful
Reserved
Resigned

Rewarding
Rhapsodic
Rhetoric
Rhetorical
Rhythmic

Rooted
Rosy
Rotten
Rotund
Rough

Rambunctious
Rampageous
Rampant
Ramrod
Ramshackle

Relentless
Relevant
Reliable
Reliant
Relieved

Resilient
Resolute
Resolved
Resonant
Resounding

Ribald
Ribbing
Rib-tickling
Rich
Rickety

Roughened
Roughhewn
Round
Roundabout
Roundly

Rancid
Rancorous
Random
Rangy
Rank

Religious
Reluctant
Remarkable
Remediable
Remedial

Resourceful
Respectable
Respected
Respectful
Resplendent

Riddled
Ridiculous
Rife
Right
Righteous

Rousing
Routine
Roving
Rowdy
Royal

Rankling	Reminiscent	Responsible	Rightful	Rubbery
Rapacious	Remiss	Responsive	Right-minded	Rubbishy
Rapid	Remittable	Restful	Right-thinking	Ruddy
Rapid-fire	Remorseful	Resting	Rigid	Rude
Rapt	Remorseless	Restive	Rigorous	Rudimentary
Rapturous	Remote	Restless	Riled	Rueful
Rare	Remotest	Restorative	Riling	Rugged
Rarified	Remunerative	Restrained	Ringing	Ruined
Raring	Renegade	Restricted	Rinky-dink	Ruinous
Rascally	Renewed	Restrictive	Riotous	Ruling
Rash	Renowned	Resultant	Ripe	Rumpled
Rasping	Reparable	Resurgent	Ripping	Rundown
Raspy	Repeated	Resuscitated	Rip-roaring	Running
Rather	Repelled	Retaliatory	Risible	Runny
Rational	Repellent	Retarded	Risky	Run-of-the-mill
Rattle-brained	Repelling	Retentive	Risqué	Rural
Rattled	Repentant	Reticent	Ritzy	Rushed
Rattling	Repetitious	Retired	Riveting	Rustic
Ratty	Repetitive	Retiring	Roaming	Rustiest
Raucous	Replete	Retrograde	Roaring	Rusty
Raunchy	Reprehensible	Revealing	Robotic	Ruthless

— S —

Saccharine	Selfish	Slanting	Spendthrift	Strident
Sacred	Self-possessed	Slap-dash	Spent	Striking
Sacrificial	Self-protective	Slaphappy	Spherical	Stringent
Sacrilegious	Self-reliant	Slapstick	Spicy	Stringy
Sacrosanct	Self-righteous	Slavering	Spiffy	Striped
Sad	Self-satisfied	Slavish	Spineless	Stripped
Saddened	Self-seeking	Sleazy	Spineless	Strong
Saddening	Self-serving	Sleek	Spine-tingling	Strong-willed
Sadistic	Self-sufficient	Sleeping	Spiny	Structural
Safe	Self-supporting	Sleepless	Spiral	Stubborn
Sagacious	Self-sustaining	Sleepy	Spirited	Stubby
Sage	Self-willed	Slender	Spiritless	Stuck
Sagging	Seminal	Slick	Spiritual	Stuck-up
Sainted	Semiprivate	Slight	Spiteful	Studded
Saintly	Semiskilled	Slightest	Splashy	Studied
Salable	Senile	Slighting	Splendid	Studious
Salacious	Senior	Slightly	Splendiferous	Stuffed
Salient	Sensational	Slim	Splenetic	Stuffy
Saline	Senseless	Slimy	Splotched	Stumbling
Sallow	Sensible	Slinky	Spoiled	Stung

Salty	Sensitive	Slippery	Spoken	Stunned
Salubrious	Sensitized	Slipshod	Spongy	Stunning
Salutary	Sensory	Slithery	Spontaneous	Stunted
Same	Sensual	Slobbering	Spooked	Stupefied
Sanctimonious	Sensuous	Sloppy	Spooky	Stupefying
Sanctioned	Sententious	Slothful	Sporadic	Stupendous
Sandy	Sentient	Slouchy	Sporting	Stupid
Sane	Sentimental	Slovenly	Sportive	Stupider
Sanguinary	Separable	Slow	Sportsmanlike	Sturdy
Sanitary	Separate	Sluggish	Spotless	Stylish
Sapped	Sequential	Slumbering	Spotted	Suave
Sanguine	Serendipitous	Slushy	Spotty	Subdued
Sappy	Serene	Sly	Spousal	Subject
Sarcastic	Serial	Small	Sprightly	Subjective
Sardonic	Serious	Smaller	Spry	Sublime
Sassy	Serpentine	Small-fry	Spunky	Subliminal
Satanic	Serrated	Small-minded	Spurious	Submerged
Sated	Serviceable	Smart	Squabble	Submissive
Satiated	Servile	Smart-alecky	Squalid	Subnormal
Satin	Settled	Smarting	Square	Subordinate
Satiny	Severe	Smashing	Squat	Subsequent
Satiric	Sexless	Smelly	Squeaky	Subservient
Satirical	Sexual	Smoggy	Squeamish	Subsidiary
Satisfactory	Sexy	Smoky	Squirrelly	Substandard
Satisfied	Shabby	Smoldering	Squishy	Substantial
Satisfying	Shaded	Smooth	Stable	Substantive
Saturated	Shadowy	Smug	Stag	Subtle
Saucy	Shady	Smutty	Staggering	Suburban
Savage	Shaggy	Snail-paced	Stagnant	Subversive
Savory	Shaky	Snaky	Stagnating	Succeeding
Saw-toothed	Shallow	Snap	Staid	Successful
Scabby	Sham	Snappily	Stained	Successive
Scabrous	Shamed	Snappish	Stainless	Succinct
Scalding	Shameful	Snappy	Stale	Succulent
Scaly	Shameless	Snarly	Stale	Sudden
Scandalous	Shapeless	Snazzy	Stalwart	Sufferable
Scant	Shared	Sneak	Stalwart	Sufficient
Scanty	Sharp	Sneaking	Standard	Suffocating
Scarce	Sharpened	Sneaky	Standing	Sugarcoated
Scared	Sharp-eyed	Snide	Standoffish	Sugary

Scary	Sharp-witted	Snippy	Star	Suggestive
Scathing	Shattering	Sniveling	Starchy	Suicidal
Scatterbrained	Shatterproof	Snobbish	Star-crossed	Suitable
Scattered	Sheepish	Snoopy	Stark	Sulky
Scenic	Sheer	Snooty	Stark	Sullen
Scented	Shell-shocked	Snotty	Starry	Sullied
Scheduled	Sheltered	Snowbound	Starry-eyed	Sultry
Scheming	Shiftless	Snug	Star-struck	Summarily
Schizophrenic	Shifty	Soaking	Startling	Sumptuous
Schlocky	Shimmering	Soapy	Starved	Sundry
Schmaltzy	Shining	Soaring	Starving	Sunken
Scholarly	Shiny	Sober	Stately	Sunlit
Scholastic	Shippable	Sociable	Stately	Sunny
Scientific	Shipshape	Sociable	State-of-art	Super
Scintillating	Shivery	Social	Static	Superabundant
Sclerotic	Shocked	Socialistic	Stationary	Superannuated
Scorching	Shocking	Sociological	Statistical	Superb
Scornful	Shoddy	Sociopathic	Statuesque	Supercharged
Scotch	Shopworn	Sodden	Statutory	Supercilious
Scottish	Shore-term	Soft	Staunch	Supercritical
Scraggly	Short	Softened	Staying	Superficial
Scrambled	Short-lived	Softhearted	Steadfast	Superfluous
Scrappy	Shortsighted	Soggy	Steady	Superhuman
Scratchy	Short-tempered	Soldierly	Stealthy	Superior
Scrawling	Showy	Sole	Steaming	Superlative
Scrawny	Shrewd	Solemn	Steamy	Supernatural
Screaming	Shrewish	Solicitous	Steely	Supersonic
Screeching	Shrieking	Solid	Steep	Superstitious
Screwball	Shrill	Solitary	Stellar	Supervisory
Screwy	Shriveled	Solo	Stereotyped	Supple
Scrimpy	Shrunken	Soluble	Stereotypical	Supplemental
Scrubby	Shuddering	Solvable	Sterile	Supplementary
Scruffy	Shy	Somber	Sterling	Supplementing
Scrumptious	Shyster	Sometime	Stern	Supplicant
Scrupulous	Sick	Sometimes	Sticky	Supported
Scummy	Sickened	Somnolent	Stiff	Supporting
Scurrilous	Sickening	Sonic	Stifling	Supportive
Scurvy	Side-splitting	Sonorous	Still	Supposed
Seamy	Sideways	Soothing	Stilted	Suppressed
Searing	Sightless	Sooty	Stimulating	Supreme

Seasick	Significant	Sophisticated	Stimulative	Sure
Seasonable	Silent	Sophomoric	Stinging	Surefire
Seasoned	Silken	Soporific	Stinging	Surefooted
Secluded	Silky	Sopping	Stingy	Surface
Secondary	Silly	Sordid	Stinking	Surfeited
Second-class	Silver	Sore	Stinky	Surly
Secondhand	Silver-tongued	Sorrowful	Stir-crazy	Surmountable
Second-rate	Silvery	Sorry	Stirring	Surpassing
Second-string	Similar	So-so	Stock	Surplus
Secret	Simpatico	Soulful	Stocky	Surprising
Secretive	Simple	Soulless	Stodgy	Surreal
Sectarian	Simpleminded	Sound	Stoic	Surreptitious
Secular	Simplistic	Soundless	Stoical	Surrounded
Secure	Simulated	Soundproof	Stolid	Susceptible
Sedate	Simultaneous	Soupy	Stone-broke	Suspect
Sedative	Sincere	Sour	Stony	Suspecting
Sedentary	Sinewy	Soused	Stopgap	Suspicious
Seditious	Sinful	Southern	Stormy	Sustainable
Seductive	Single	Sovereign	Stout	Svelte
Seedy	Singular	Space-age	Stouthearted	Swaggering
Seeming	Sinister	Spaced-out	Straight	Swanky
Seemliest	Sinuous	Spacious	Straightaway	Swarming
Seemly	Sissified	Spare	Straight-faced	Swarthy
Seldom	Situated	Sparing	Straightforward	Swashbuckling
Select	Sizeable	Sparkling	Strained	Sweaty
Selective	Sizzling	Sparky	Strait-laced	Sweeping
Self-appointed	Skeletal	Sparse	Strange	Sweet
Self-assertive	Skeptical	Spartan	Strapping	Swell
Self-assured	Sketchy	Spasmodic	Strategic	Sweltering
Self-centered	Skewed	Spastic	Stratospheric	Swift
Self-conceited	Skillful	Special	Stray	Swinging
Self-confident	Skimpy	Specialized	Streaked	Swinish
Self-conscious	Skin-deep	Specific	Streaky	Swollen
Self-contained	Skinny	Specious	Streamlined	Symbolic
Self-destructive	Skittish	Speckled	Street-smart	Sympathetic
Self-effacing	Skuzzy	Spectacular	Strenuous	Symptomatic
Self-evident	Sky-high	Speculative	Stressed-out	Synergistic
Self-explanatory	Slack	Speechless	Stressful	Synthetic
Self-fulfilling	Slackened	Speedy	Stretchable	Syrupy
Self-glorifying	Slanderous	Spellbinding	Stretched	Systematic
Self-governing	Slanted	Spellbound	Strict	Systemic

— T —

Taboo	Tempestuous	Thoroughgoing	Tongue-tied	Tremendous
Tacit	Temporal	Thoughtful	Toothsome	Tremulous
Taciturn	Temporary	Thoughtless	Top-drawer	Trenchant
Tacky	Tempting	Threadbare	Topical	Trendy
Tactful	Tenable	Threatening	Top-level	Triangular
Tactical	Tenacious	Thriftless	Topmost	Tricky
Tactless	Tender	Thrifty	Top-notch	Trifling
Tailored	Tenderhearted	Thrilling	Topsy-turvy	Trim
Tailor-made	Tending	Thriving	Tormented	Trite
Tainted	Tense	Thronging	Tormenting	Triumphant
Taking	Tentative	Through	Torpid	Trivial
Talented	Tenuous	Thunderous	Torrential	Tropical
Talkative	Tepid	Thunderstruck	Torrid	Troubled
Talky	Terminal	Tickled	Tortuous	Troublesome
Tall	Terminated	Ticklish	Torturing	Troubling
Tame	Terminating	Tidied	Total	Truant
Tangential	Terrible	Tidy	Totalitarian	Truculent
Tangible	Terrific	Tight	Touchable	True-blue
Tangled	Terrified	Tight-fisted	Touching	Trustful
Tantalizing	Terrifying	Tightlipped	Touchy	Trusting
Tantamount	Terse	Tilting	Tough	Trustworthy
Tardy	Tested	Timeless	Tousled	Trusty
Tart	Testy	Timely	Towering	Truthful
Tasteful	Thankful	Timid	Toxic	Trying
Tasteless	Thankless	Timorous	Tractable	Tubby
Tasty	Thawed	Tiny	Traditional	Tubular
Tattered	Theatrical	Tipped	Tragic	Tumbledown
Taunting	Theoretical	Tipsy	Traitorous	Tumultuous
Taut	Therapeutic	Tip-top	Tranquil	Turbocharged
Tawdry	Therefore	Tired	Tranquilizing	Turbulent
Taxing	Thermal	Tireless	Transcendental	Turgid
Tearful	Thermonuclear	Tiresome	Transient	Tweedy
Teary	Thick	Tiring	Transitory	Twin
Technical	Thick-headed	Titanic	Translucent	Twin-sized
Tedious	Thick-skinned	Titillating	Transmittable	Twisted
Teeming	Thick-witted	Titular	Transparent	Twisting
Teeny	Thin	Together	Trapped	Twitchy
Teeny-weeny	Thinking	Toilsome	Trashy	Two-faced
Teetotal	Thin-skinned	Tolerable	Traumatic	Twofold
Telling	Thirsty	Tolerant	Treacherous	Typical

Telltale	Thorny	Tolerating	Treasured	Tyrannical
Temperamental	Thorough	Toned-down	Trembling	Tyrannous
Temperate	Thoroughbred	Tongue-in-cheek		

— U —

Ubiquitous	Underground	Unimpressed	Unscrupulous
Uglier	Uncovered	Unimpressive	Unseasonable
Ugliest	Uncritical	Unimproved	Unseasoned
Ugly	Unctuous	Uninhabited	Unseat
Ulcerative	Uncultivated	Uninhibited	Unseeing
Ulterior	Undamaged	Uninitiated	Unseemly
Ultimate	Undaunted	Uninjured	Unseen
Ultra	Undecided	Uninspired	Unselective
Ultraconservative	Undeclared	Uninspiring	Unselfish
Ultramarine	Undefeated	Unintelligent	Unsettled
Ultramodern	Undefined	Unintelligible	Unshackled
Ultrasonic	Undemocratic	Unintended	Unshaken
Umber	Undemonstrative	Unintentional	Unsheltered
Umbilical	Undeniable	Uninterested	Unshielded
Umbrage	Undependable	Uninteresting	Unsightly
Unabated	Under	Uninterrupted	Unsigned
Unable	Underage	Uninvited	Unskilled
Unabridged	Underappreciated	Uninviting	Unsold
Unacceptable	Undercover	Uninvolved	Unsolicited
Unacceptable	Undercut	Unique	Unsolved
Unaccompanied	Underdeveloped	Unisex	Unsophisticated
Unaccomplished	Underestimated	Unjust	Unsound
Unaccountable	Underhanded	Unjustifiable	Unspeakable
Unaccustomed	Underlying	Unjustified	Unspecified
Unachievable	Underneath	Unkempt	Unspoiled
Unacknowledged	Undernourished	Unkind	Unspoken
Unacquainted	Underpaid	Unknowing	Unsportsmanlike
Unadjusted	Underprivileged	Unknown	Unstable
Unadorned	Underrated	Unlawful	Unsteady
Unadulterated	Undersized	Unlicensed	Unstructured
Unadvised	Understandable	Unlike	Unstrung
Unaffected	Understanding	Unlikely	Unstuck
Unafraid	Understated	Unlimited	Unsubstantial
Unaided	Understood	Unlisted	Unsubstantiated
Unaligned	Undervalued	Unloving	Unsuccessful

Unalike	Underweight	Unlucky	Unsuitable
Unalterable	Underwhelmed	Unmanageable	Unsullied
Unambiguous	Undeserved	Unmanly	Unsung
Un-American	Undesirable	Unmarked	Unsupervised
Unanimated	Undetectable	Unmarried	Unsupportable
Unanimous	Undiplomatic	Unmatched	Unsure
Unanswered	Undisciplined	Unmentionable	Unsurpassable
Unanticipated	Undisclosed	Unmerciful	Unsurpassed
Unapologetic	Undisputed	Unmeritorious	Unsuspecting
Unappealing	Undisturbed	Unmet	Unsuspicious
Unappetizing	Undoubted	Unmistakable	Unsustainable
Unappreciated	Undue	Unmitigated	Unswerving
Unappreciative	Undulating	Unmotivated	Unsympathetic
Unapproachable	Undying	Unmoving	Untainted
Unarmed	Unearned	Unnamed	Untalented
Unashamed	Uneasy	Unnatural	Untamed
Unasked	Unbeaten	Unnecessary	Untapped
Unassailable	Uneducated	Unneeded	Untarnished
Unassimilated	Unembellished	Unnerving	Untenable
Unassisted	Unemotional	Unnoticed	Untested
Unassuming	Unemployed	Unnumbered	Unthankful
Unattached	Unencumbered	Unobtainable	Unthinkable
Unattainable	Unending	Unobtrusive	Unthinking
Unattended	Unendurable	Unoccupied	Untidy
Unattractive	Unenforceable	Unofficial	Untimely
Unauthorized	Unenlightened	Unopened	Untiring
Unavailable	Unenthusiastic	Unorthodox	Untold
Unavailing	Unenviable	Unpaid	Untouchable
Unavoidable	Unequal	Unparalleled	Untouched
Unaware	Unequalled	Unparalleled	Untrained
Unbalanced	Unequivocal	Unpatriotic	Untried
Unbearable	Unerring	Unpaved	Untroubled
Unbeatable	Unessential	Unperceived	Untrue
Unbeaten	Unethical	Unperturbed	Untrustworthy
Unbecoming	Uneven	Unplanned	Untutored
Unbeknownst	Uneventful	Unpleasant	Unused
Unbelievable	Unexciting	Unpolished	Unutterable
Unbelieving	Unexpected	Unpopular	Unvarnished
Unbending	Unexplainable	Unprecedented	Unvarying
Unbiased	Unexplored	Unpredictable	Unverified